THE 'THREE NIGHTS' BLITZ'

Frontispiece. Fighting the fires in Ben Evans's department store. *SAO.*

THE 'THREE NIGHTS' BLITZ'

Select Contemporary Reports relating to Swansea's Air Raids of February 1941

J.R. Alban

CITY OF SWANSEA

1994

First published 1994 by Swansea City Council.
Obtainable from the City Archives Office, Central Services Department, Guildhall, Swansea, SA1 4PE.

City Archives Publications: Studies in Swansea's History, no. 3.

ISBN 0 946001 25 1

General Editor:
J.R. Alban, B.A., Ph.D., D.A.A., *City Archivist*.

Contents

	Page
List of Illustrations.	vii
Abbreviations.	ix
General Editor's Preface.	xi
Acknowledgements.	xiii
Introduction.	xv
Chapter 1: The Air Raids on Swansea, 1940–3.	1
Chapter 2: The 'Three Nights' Blitz'.	13
Chapter 3: The Organization of Civil Defence in Swansea.	22
Chapter 4: *Luftwaffe* Units involved in the 'Three Nights' Blitz'.	30
Chapter 5: German Aircraft involved in the 'Three Nights' Blitz'.	35
Chapter 6: German Bombs dropped on Swansea.	41
Introduction to the Documents:	45
Document 1. Official List of Air Attacks on Swansea, 1940-3, compiled by the County Borough of Swansea Air Raid Precautions Department.	47
Document 2. German Operations Reports on the 'Three Nights' Blitz' on Swansea.	49
Document 3. County Borough of Swansea Auxiliary Fire Service Summary Reports relating to the 'Three Nights' Blitz'.	55
Document 4. Select Press Reports on the 'Three Nights' Blitz'.	57
Document 5. Official Report on the 'Three Nights' Blitz' by Mr Howell Lang Lang-Coath, Air Raid Precautions Controller for Swansea.	59
Document 6. Mass-Observation Report on Swansea after the 'Three Nights' Blitz'.	63

		Page
Texts of the Documents:		67
Document 1.	Official List of Air Attacks on Swansea, 1940-3, compiled by the County Borough of Swansea Air Raid Precautions Department.	69
Document 2.	German Operations Reports on the 'Three Nights' Blitz' on Swansea.	74
Document 3.	County Borough of Swansea Auxiliary Fire Service Summary Reports relating to the 'Three Nights' Blitz'.	106
Document 4.	Select Press Reports on the 'Three Nights' Blitz'.	131
Document 5.	Official Report on the 'Three Nights' Blitz' by Mr Howell Lang Lang-Coath, Air Raid Precautions Controller for Swansea.	148
Document 6.	Mass-Observation Report on Swansea after the 'Three Nights' Blitz'.	163
Bibliography.		173

List of Illustrations

		Page
Frontispiece.	Fighting the fires in Ben Evans's department store.	ii
Figure 1.	Swansea town centre before the blitz.	2
Figure 2.	German target plan of Swansea based on an aerial reconaissance photograph.	5
Figure 3.	Three-dimensional German model of Swansea.	8
Figure 4.	German view of Swansea docks from the air.	9
Figure 5.	Fires rage in central Swansea on 21 February 1941. The only known photograph of the 'Three Nights' Blitz' in progress.	14
Figure 6.	Fighting the fires in Ben Evans's department store, from Wind Street.	15
Figure 7.	Royal Engineers bomb disposal team at YMCA canteen in High Street.	16
Figure 8.	Damaged houses in Teilo Crescent, Mayhill.	17
Figure 9.	College Street and Gower Street, looking west.	18
Figure 10.	Castle Street and College Street junction, looking south.	19
Figure 11.	Aerial view showing the extent of damage in central Swansea.	20
Figure 12.	ARP Divisions after March 1939.	23
Figure 13.	AFS officers at a Canadian mobile canteen outside the Guildhall.	25
Figure 14.	Layout of Gun Site 'T' at King George V Playing Fields.	27
Figure 15.	ARP workers in the ruins of David Evans's store.	29
Figure 16.	Bases of *Luftwaffe* units involved in the 'Three Nights' Blitz'.	31

		Page
Figure 17.	Heinkel He. 111s.	36
Figure 18.	Dornier Do. 17.	37
Figure 19.	Junkers Ju. 88.	37
Figure 20.	Types of German high explosive bombs from an ARP manual.	42
Figure 21.	German incendiary bomb, type B1 E1 ZA, dropped on Swansea during the 'Three Nights' Blitz'.	44
Figure 22.	German incendiary bomb container AB 36 which held thirty-six B1 E1 incendiary bombs.	44
Figure 23.	A daylight raid on Llandarcy oil refinery, probably on 10 July 1940.	46
Figure 24.	German aerial photograph of a raid in progress on Llandarcy oil refinery, probably on 10 July 1940.	48
Figure 25.	Page from a German Operations Report.	50
Figure 26.	German target map of Swansea, 1941.	52–3
Figure 27.	AFS personnel in the ruins of Swansea market.	55
Figure 28.	Howell Lang Lang-Coath, ARP Controller.	60
Figure 29.	Alderman Percy Morris, Chairman of the ARP Committee.	62
Figure 30.	A policeman surveys the ruins of Castle Street.	64
Figure 31.	Insignia of some German bomber units involved in the 'Three Nights' Blitz'.	66
Front cover.	Damage at the junction of Oxford Street and Goat Street looking west, 21 February 1941.	

Abbreviations

AB 36	German designation for a cylindrical canister, dropped from an aircraft, and containing thirty-six B1 E1 (*q.v.*) incendiary bombs.
AFS	Auxiliary Fire Service.
ARP	Air Raid Precautions.
B1 El	German designation *(Brandbombe 1 Kilogram Elektron)* for incendiary bomb of 1 kilogram.
B1 El ZA	German designation for incendiary bomb of 1 kilogram, with explosive detonator.
Do. 17	Dornier 17 bomber.
H.E.	High explosive bomb.
He. 111	Heinkel 111 bomber.
H.T.	Heavy trailer pump used by the AFS.
I.B.	Incendiary bomb.
Ju. 88	Junkers 88 bomber.
K.G.	*Kampfgeschwade*r, a bomber wing.
K.Gr.	*Kampfgruppe*, a unit forming part of a *Kampfgeschwader*, or else a specialist bomber unit such as a pathfinder group.
L.T.	Light trailer pump used by the AFS.
LZZ	German designation *(Lange Zeit Zunder)* for a high explosive bomb with a delayed action fuse.
NFS	National Fire Service.
P.M.	Parachute mine.
PRO	Public Record Office, London.
SAO	Swansea City Archives Office.

SC	German designation *(Spreng Cylindrisch)* for a thin-walled, high explosive bomb. The prefix was followed by a number which indicated the bomb's weight in kilograms.
SD	German designation *(Spreng Dickenwand)* for a thick-walled, high explosive fragmentation bomb.
SWEP	*South Wales Evening Post.*
U.X. or U.X.B.	Unexploded bomb.
WGRO	West Glamorgan County Archive Service, Swansea.

General Editor's Preface

The production of this book, the third in Swansea City Archives Office's series, 'Studies in Swansea's History', has placed a dual burden on the General Editor of the series, who is also the author of the book. However, involvement in these twin capacities, while bringing with it twice the work, has, he feels, also brought double the creative pleasure.

'Studies in Swansea's History' has now established itself as a respected series of scholarly works on Swansea, and it is hoped that this present volume will maintain the tradition. The two earlier volumes were principally concerned with aspects of Swansea's social history. The present study also contains a large amount of social history, but to this are added elements of military, and, indeed, international history. In fact, as a subject, the 'Three Nights' Blitz' has always aroused a great deal of interest, and the documents printed in this book were therefore deemed to be fitting material for inclusion in the present series.

The author, who has held the post of City Archivist since 1974, has been carrying on his own research into aspects of the history of Swansea for twenty years. Originally specialising in military history (albeit of the medieval period) he has had a long-standing interest in Swansea during the Second World War and, indeed, between 1975 and 1981, headed a research project into the air raids on Swansea.

As the author states in his introduction, many questions have been asked about the 'Three Nights' Blitz' on Swansea. This book does not profess to give answers to all those questions, but by printing in full the texts of six contemporary reports, it is hoped that readers will be permitted to come to their own conclusions about an extremely significant episode in Swansea's history.

J.R. Alban

Acknowledgements

Many individuals and institutions have been consulted during the preparation of this volume. Thanks are due to the *Bundesarchiv/ Militärarchiv*, Freiburg and to the Swansea Press Ltd. for permission to publish texts of documents, and also to Mr Laurie Latchford for allowing reference to his war-time diaries held in the Swansea City Archives Office. The text of Document 6 is Copyright the Trustees of the Mass-Observation Archive at the University of Sussex, reproduced by permission of Curtis Brown Group Ltd., London. Acknowledgement is also made to Barnaby's Picture Library and to Topham Picture Source for permission to reproduce photographs of German bombers.

I am also grateful to the staffs of the following organizations: Bristol City Record Office, Devonshire County Library Service, Devonshire County Record Office, Dorset County Record Office, the Imperial War Museum, Portsmouth City Record Office, the Public Record Office, Kew, the RAF Museum, Hendon (especially to Mr Ben Travers of the Research Department), Somerset County Record Office, Southampton City Record Office, the Model Shop, Swansea, and, in particular, to the staff of the Swansea City Archives Office, who have not only had to cope with me as a colleague, but as a researcher as well.

There are a number of individuals who are deserving of my thanks, among them, Miss Susan Beckley, County Archivist of West Glamorgan, and Professor Rhys W. Williams of the University College of Swansea. Especial thanks are due to Mr K.W.B. Lightfoot and Frau Susanne Lightfoot, of the University of Lüneburg, and to Herr Kurt Fischer, formerly of the *Luftwaffe*.

In restating my gratitude to all the above, may I say that without their help and advice, this book would not have been written. However, any errors of omission or commission which appear in this work are entirely my responsibility.

I am deeply indebted to Swansea City Council which, through its Policy and Resources Committee, has supported the 'Studies in Swansea's History' series. Without such enlightened support these contributions towards the history of Swansea, which have been further facilitated by the City Council's maintenance of a City Archives Office, would not have come into print.

Last, but by no means least, I must thank my wife, Pamela, and my sons, Richard, Timothy, and Nicholas, for their tolerance in 'living through the blitz' during the period when I was writing this book.

Introduction

During the Second World War the important port and industrial town of Swansea was attacked from the air on about forty occasions. There is some confusion as to the precise number of raids, stemming largely from the fact that in many instances it was often difficult to define what actually constituted a raid. The town was under warning on 524 occasions, but only a few of these were actually deemed to be raids. The main criterion was whether bombs were dropped or not, and in most cases the threatening aircraft moved on towards other targets. Indeed, in many instances, what was considered to be a 'raid' on Swansea was often a casc of aircraft, intended for another target, jettisoning bombs in the vicinity of the town. Some such incidents were minor and when bombs were dropped into the sea or on the rural periphery of Swansea, or, indeed, in that 'no man's land' near the boundary of two ARP districts, then the incident did not always merit a mention in Swansea's officially compiled records. Thus, the Swansea Air Raid Precautions Department's official list of raids on Swansea, printed in this edition, gives the total number of raids as thirty-nine. Subsequent secondary sources have given variations of this total. For instance, K. Pryer's list ('compiled from official sources') published in *Luftwaffe over Swansea* (Swansea, n.d.) gives the total as forty-four, while N. Arthur in *Swansea at War. A Pictorial Account, 1939-45* (Manchester, 1988) suggests a total of forty-five. Nevertheless, when bombs did actually fall on Swansea, the raids varied greatly in extent: from mere jettisoning of loads, to hit and run attacks by individual aircraft, to six large and severe blitzes. While it was the blitzes which caused the greatest material damage, all the attacks left their mark on the face of the town and on the lives of the inhabitants.

Although Swansea sustained a large number of attacks during a period which lasted just under two and a half years, it is the so-called 'Three Nights' Blitz' of 19, 20, and 21 February 1941 which is most usually recalled whenever the air raids on Swansea are discussed by Swansea people. Indeed, for many persons looking back, it seems that the 'Three

Nights' Blitz' are the only raids ever recounted. This is perhaps not surprising, since the enemy action of those three nights in February 1941 caused the most severe damage and disruption of all the attacks on Swansea. They resulted in the devastation of forty-one acres of the town centre and casualties amounting to 639, of whom 230 were killed. Moreover, they left a blemish on the face of central Swansea which was not wholly eradicated until the rebuilding of the town centre was completed in the early 1960s. Even so, the modern appearance of central Swansea today is still a permanent reminder that a change has taken place there, a change necessitated by the violent destruction of air raids during the Second World War.

The 'Three Nights' Blitz' is an episode in Swansea's history about which supposedly every local schoolchild knows. But when one digs deeply to investigate it one finds that the subject is fraught with question marks, and is often clouded by myth and rumour. The relatively poor survival rate of primary sources relating to Swansea's blitz has exacerbated this situation, and wartime censorship practices compounded it. However, since the mid 1970s, much new research into Swansea during the Second World War has been going on, particularly with regard to the air raids, and there has been a growing number of publications on the subject. There are, nevertheless, many questions still to be answered. This edition prints a selected series of contemporary British and German documents about the 'Three Nights' Blitz'. With the exception of the press reports, none of them has previously been published in its entirety. It is hoped that they will, in part, help to throw some further light on a subject which has been described as 'the most significant event in Swansea's recent history'.

CHAPTER 1

The Air Raids on Swansea, 1940–3

At the beginning of the Second World War, Swansea was a sizeable south Wales town of 167,000 inhabitants. Situated at the mouth of the river Tawe and on the Bristol Channel, it was ideally located for international maritime trade. In the course of the nineteenth and early twentieth centuries, a great system of five docks had been established to support that trade, making Swansea one of the most important of western ports.[1] Indeed, during the Second World War, when war supplies began to arrive from north America, Swansea was one of the principal British ports for receipt of such goods.[2]

The town was also a major industrial centre, with the bulk of its works located in the Lower Swansea Valley, a short distance to the north of the town centre, although there were also some factories situated near the docks and to the east of the town, where the Tir John North power station and Llandarcy oil refinery were also located. Since the eighteenth century, Swansea had been a major centre for the refining of copper, and in the nineteenth century a host of other metallurgical industries, including tinplate, zinc, lead, and steel tube fabrication, together with numerous subsidiary industries, had been established there. There was also a large coal exporting trade, consisting mainly of anthracite from the north-western rim of the south Wales coalfield, while Swansea was also a major centre for the manufacture of patent fuel, a coal derivative.[3]

By the first decades of the twentieth century, several of these industries were beginning to show signs of decline, but at the beginning of the Second World War, Swansea was still an important industrial and commercial town.[4] It was also a major centre of population and, in a sense, a regional capital for south-west Wales. Moreover, it lay on an important railway network, the line passing to the north of the town at Landore being the main railway connexion with London and west Wales. In pre-war discussions, Swansea had been identified as a major potential target for enemy air attacks, and when war came, the town's docks were to prove critical in the Battle of the Atlantic, its metallurgical industries and coal crucial to the war effort.[5] Indeed, in the years immediately prior to the outbreak of war, new industries, such as munitions, had been established in the Lower Swansea Valley, making the town an even more legitimate target for the bomber. However, the pattern of actual attacks on Swansea, in the main, spared the industries and dock installations, and struck at residential and commercial areas.

Figure 1. Swansea town centre before the blitz. *SAO.*

The forty or so air raids which Swansea suffered during the Second World War varied enormously in intensity. Many were fairly light raids by small numbers of aircraft or individual aircraft, although there were six heavier attacks or 'blitzes' which caused severe damage. In fact, several of the lesser attacks may not have been intended by the Germans as raids on

Swansea at all. They were possibly instances of aircraft, scheduled for attacks on other targets, which, for whatever reason, jettisoned their bombs in the vicinity of Swansea. For example, the dropping of incendiaries and high explosive bombs at Limeslade and Thistleboon on 8 April 1941 was certainly such a case: two He. 111s of *Kampfgruppe 100*, originally destined for Greenock in Scotland, flew off course due to bad weather, and attacked Swansea as an alternative target.[6] The incident which occurred just after midnight on 3 August 1940, when high explosive bombs were dropped in the sea off Mumbles Head, was probably also such a case. German sources do not indicate planned attacks on Swansea for that night or, indeed, for many other occasions on which Swansea was attacked.

Although war was declared in September 1939, Swansea, like many other British towns, was spared attack from the air for many months. Indeed, the 'Phoney War' period did much to reinforce the idea that the town lay outside the range of German bombers and that it would not be attacked. Therefore, pre-war ARP measures were deemed by many to have been a waste of time and money. In fact, while German medium range bombers were still stationed at airfields in Germany, Swansea was too far away for them to attack and return safely to base. However, with the fall of France in the early summer of 1940, and the capture by the Germans of airfields on the Channel coast and in Brittany, Swansea came well within the range of the *Luftwaffe*. It is therefore no coincidence that the first air raids on Swansea occurred in June 1940, shortly after the fall of France.[7]

The air raids on Swansea may be divided into two principal phases, with two later attacks lying outside those two main periods. Precise details of the attacks will be found in the official list of Air Raids on Swansea, 1940–3 which is reproduced as Document 1 below.[8]

The first phase of air attacks began on 27 June 1940 and came to an end on the following 21 October. Most of the raids in this period were minor, several of the earliest ones being in the daytime. The first attack of all, however, occurred at 3.30 a.m. on the morning of 27 June 1940, when a stick of six high explosive bombs fell on Danygraig and Kilvey Hill. A house at Danygraig Road was damaged and some of the bombs failed to explode. No warning was given for this raid, which may well have been an instance of a single aircraft jettisoning its bombs by chance over Swansea. The second raid, in the early morning of 29 June, resulted in two high explosive bombs falling near the Upper Fforest tinplate works at Morriston, with no casualties or damage.

It was in the third raid of the war that Swansea sustained its first casualties. This was an enigmatic daytime attack on 10 July by an aircraft bearing French military markings. The intruder appeared without warning, and although it was observed from many quarters, it flew over the town without challenge, and at 10.20 a.m. commenced its run in over the King's Dock, where it dropped four high explosive bombs. The result was extensive damage to sheds and warehouses at the Mole end of the dock, with twelve dockers being killed and twenty-six injured. There is no record of this attack among the surviving German sources, and the provenance of the aircraft and the composition of its crew remain a mystery to this day.

Daylight raids also occurred on 30 July and 18 August. However, most of Swansea's raids were night attacks, and all raids after 18 August were carried out under cover of darkness. Indeed, in August and September, the frequency and intensity of attacks on Swansea increased. For instance, on 10 August, the railway line and viaduct at Landore appear to have been targets, with about thirty bombs falling in the vicinity of the viaduct and also on the adjoining districts of Brynhyfryd, Landore, and Manselton. Several bombs, including thirteen which failed to explode, also landed in the Singleton, Clyne, and Ravenhill areas. In this raid, fifteen people were killed and a further fifteen injured. Some casualties were also sustained in raids on 2, 17, and 18 August, but the grimmest casualty list to date occurred as the result of the first blitz on the town, on the night of 1–2 September. In this raid 106 high explosive bombs and over 1,000 incendiaries fell over various parts of the town, causing extensive damage and resulting in 33 deaths and 108 persons being injured.

There were six more attacks in September, the final raids being small ones and the bomb loads dropped suggesting attacks by individual aircraft. Although these caused some damage, there were no casualties. Swansea's first phase of raids ended with that of 21 October, the end of the Battle of Britain bringing some respite, as the German *Luftwaffe* regrouped. Nevertheless, several British industrial towns were attacked throughout November and December 1940, although Swansea was not selected as a target.

Figure 2. German target plan of Swansea based on an aerial reconaissance photograph. *SAO.*

Translation:

A. GB *50 56* *Power Station Tir John North:* 1) Engine- and boiler house about 4,800 sq. metres. 2) Switch house about 350 sq. metres. 3) Open air installation about 4,500 sq. metres. 4) Adjoining buildings about 150 sq. metres, built on area about 9,800 sq. metres, total area about 33,00 sq. metres.

B. GB 71 21 *Magnesium Works:* 1) Shop with reduction furnace and pumping installation about 3,400 sq. metres. 2) Refinery about 300 sq. metres. 3) Smelting shop about 300 sq. metres 4) Boiler house and steam generator about 300 sq. metres. 5) 4 storage tanks about 5–13 metres. 6) Adjoining buildings about 700 sq. metres, built on area about 6,000 sq. metres, total area about 30,000 sq. metres.

From January 1941, the *Luftwaffe* began to concentrate its force against the Battle of the Atlantic ports, of which Swansea was one. Thus, between 2 January and 19 November 1941 there were nineteen separate attacks on Swansea. Again, many of these raids were minor ones, but in January and especially February 1941 there were concerted, heavy offensives against the town. The first three raids, however, on 2, 4, and 13 January, were light ones, but on the 17th of the month there occurred Swansea's second blitz. The first warning of the raid was given at 7.10 p.m. and the final all clear at 4.06 a.m. the following morning. This was, in fact, the heaviest *single* raid which Swansea sustained during the Second World War. Eighty-eight aircraft were involved and in the course of nine hours, 89 tonnes of high explosive bombs and between 6,000 and 7,000 incendiaries fell over a widespread area of the town, causing greatest damage in St Thomas, Bonymaen, and Hafod. The raid resulted in a relatively high level of casualties, with fifty-five killed and ninety-seven injured. The rescue operations were hampered by the heavy snow which had fallen a few days before the raid, and, indeed, several of the casualties were not discovered until the snow had thawed a few days later. Among the victims of this raid was the wife of Alderman Percy Morris, the Chairman of Swansea's ARP Committee.

Swansea then had a respite of just over a month until the next attacks, the 'Three Nights' Blitz' of 19, 20, and 21 February 1941. The most severe successive raids of the war for Swansea, the 'Three Nights' Blitz' and their long and short term results were devastating. They are described in more detail in the next chapter. Fortunately for Swansea, there were no further raids until early in March, and the twelve remaining attacks of 1941 were all minor ones.

On 2 July 1942, in an isolated attack, a lone raider dropped a load of incendiary bombs in the Birchgrove area, with no damage or casualties. This appears not to have been a concerted raid on Swansea, but was probably an aircraft jettisoning its bomb load. However, a far more serious attack occurred on 16 February 1943 when a prolonged blitz took place. In this final raid on the town, the residential areas of Brynmill, Hafod, and St Thomas were badly affected, with considerable damage and relatively high casualties: thirty-four killed and 110 injured. Although the effect of this raid was mainly against civilians, German press reports about it claimed quite untruthfully that it struck against docks and industry.[9] Indeed, very few of the raids on Swansea actually hit legitimate military targets such as industries and communications. The majority of bombs actually fell on residential and commercial areas, where their main results were severe disruption of the usual daily routine, creation of uncertainty and fear, all of which resulted in an adverse effect on morale.

That is not to say that a precise objective, such as the destruction of morale, was the avowed intention of the German airforce in any of the raids on Swansea. There had, of course, been precise aims mentioned in several of Hitler's early war directives, which applied to Swansea. For instance, Directive no. 9, of 29 November 1939, which concerned actions against the economy of the enemy, included Swansea among the ten most important 'English' ports, being crucial, among other things, for the export of coal. This directive stipulated that

> it is particularly important, in the harbours of Leith, Sunderland, Hull, Grimsby, London, Manchester (Ship Canal), Liverpool, Cardiff, Swansea, Bristol-Avonmouth, to destroy the large sea-locks upon which, particularly on the west coast, the regulation of the water level, and thus the effectiveness of the ports, depends.[10]

By the early months of 1941, the *Luftwaffe's* main activities in the west were clearly directed at the 'Battle of the Atlantic' ports, Directive no. 23 of 6 February 1941 stating that

> it will therefore be desirable in future to concentrate air attacks more closely and to deliver them chiefly against targets whose destruction supplements our naval war .... For this purpose it will be necessary ... to destroy the most important English harbours for imports, particularly port installations, and ships lying in them or building.[11]

This reinforced a dictated memorandum of 4 February which indicated that, among other things, there was to be a concentration of bombing on dock installations and industries, and which named the ports of Kingston upon Hull, Southampton, the mouth of the Tyne, the southern coast of the Bristol Channel, Cardiff, Liverpool, Manchester, Middlesborough, Clyde-Glasgow, and Swansea.[12]

Despite these seemingly clear aims, the main thrust of the attacks on Swansea, and particularly of the 'Three Nights' Blitz', was actually delivered on civilian rather than industrial areas. However, this again was in keeping with previously stated German objectives. In the 1930s, the tactician, Dr Robert Knauss[13] had stated that civilian morale was to be a major target of any future bombing offensive, and, while in their own press

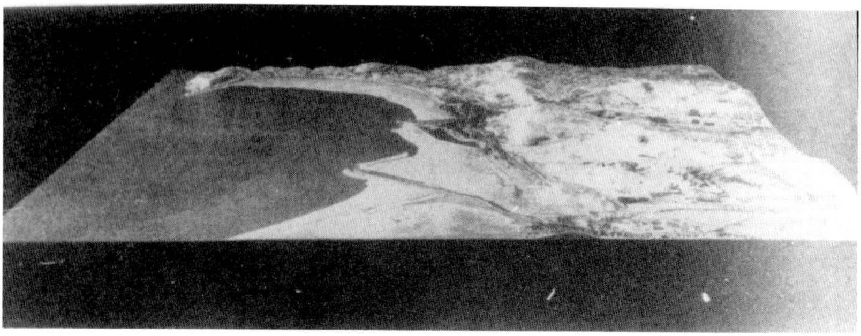

135. **Modelluftbild von Swansea** von O.
Deutlich erkennbar der Höhenzug im N. der Stadt. — Abschnitt 25.

Figure 3. Three-dimensional German model of Swansea, from *Militärgeographische Angaben über England. Westküste — Südliche Teil (Von Cornwall bis Anglesey), Abgeschlossen am 27 Dezember 1940 (Generalstab des Heeres,* Berlin, 1941). *SAO.*

releases the Germans denied this to be the case, it is clear that they continued to accept the wisdom of Knauss's philosophy.

Post-war commentators have been puzzled by the pattern of bombing strikes on Swansea and several reasons have been postulated to explain why the Germans hit the town centre rather than the docks or industries. One popular explanation was that Kilvey Hill, looming high above the East Side, prevented bombers from flying directly over the docks. The German operations reports, however, show quite clearly that in all the major blitzes, the hostile aircraft attacked from altitudes greatly in excess of 600 feet, the height of Kilvey Hill. Another widely-believed explanation was that the bombing aids which the Germans used were only accurate to within 500 metres of either side of the direction-finding beam which was used. Thus, a beam laid directly over the docks would be within 500 metres of the town centre and any such inaccuracy would result in this area's being hit. This theory cannot, however, be substantiated.

The fact was that in the early 1940s, despite the availability of *Knickebein* and other bombing aids, aircraft bombing at night and from fairly high altitudes were just not accurate enough to pinpoint targets precisely. The German raid reports for the 'Three Nights' Blitz' and the other attacks on Swansea do not usually specify particular objectives within the town. For them, the target was Swansea itself — *Zielraum Swansea* —

so if bombs fell anywhere in this area they were on target. Thus, if factories, railways, or the docks were hit, the attack would have been successful in having damaged the enemy's war production; if bombs landed on residential and commercial areas, the potential victim would have been the enemy's morale.

It is clear that, as a result of the numerous air raids between June 1940 and February 1943, Swansea suffered heavy material damage and fairly heavy loss of life. By the end of the period, 387 people had died and 851 persons had been injured, most of the casualties and material damage having resulted from the six blitzes. Indeed, one can say that the majority of attacks against Swansea were relatively minor, and only a small proportion of them were premeditated. These include the six blitzes, some of the daytime raids of summer 1940, and some of the early night raids from the same period. Yet, in one sense, all the raids were successful in that they caused fear and disruption, even if only the larger raids resulted in significant material and personal damage.

133. **Hafen von Swansea.**
Prince of Wales, King's und Queen's Docks. Links die Mündung des Tawe. Blick von SW. - Abschnitt 25.

Figure 4. German view of Swansea docks from the air. *SAO.*

However, even the larger raids on Swansea were not officially considered to be 'major attacks'. Both the German *Luftwaffe* and the British authorities defined a 'major raid' as one in which more than 100 tonnes of high explosive bombs were dropped.[14] The German air raid documents show that in none of the attacks on Swansea was anything like that quantity dropped. The 'Three Nights' Blitz' saw 49.2, 58.4 and 47.6 tonnes dropped on successive nights respectively, while even in Swansea's heaviest individual raid, the blitz of 17 January 1941, only 89 tonnes were dropped.[15] To put this into its perspective, on each of the last four nights of August 1940, Merseyside received more than 100 tonnes, while on the night of 14/15 November 1940, 500 tonnes fell on Coventry in a raid which obliterated the city centre, killed 554 persons, and seriously wounded 865, a figure which exceeded the total for all the raids on Swansea combined. Swansea's heaviest attacks, in official terminology, were classed only as 'other large raids', that is to say, raids in which between fifty and 100 tonnes of high explosive bombs were dropped. However, in terms of material damage, Swansea suffered heavily, and the effects of the raids were still to be seen well into the 1950s, and even the early 1960s, for it took many years for the town centre to be rebuilt. By the end of the war, 27,450 properties in the County Borough of Swansea had been damaged in some way, 13,927 of them seriously, while 2,000 properties had been completely destroyed. The most noticeable legacy was the devastation of the town centre, caused mainly by the 'Three Nights' Blitz', which is described in greater detail below. While there had been about forty actual raids, the warning sirens had sounded 524 times, the last occasion being on 14 May 1944. Many of these instances had been false alarms or occasions when raiders flew over Swansea on their way to targets further north. Nevertheless, the impact of these alarms clearly had their effect on civilian morale, especially when one considers that the town was on the alert for a total of 1,537 hours in a four-year period.

If the raids on Swansea were officially regarded as not being major ones, one should not underestimate their impact on the locality. Swansea's casualty figures may not have equalled those of some English cities, such as London and Coventry, but they were the highest of any place in Wales. In the Principality, 958 persons were killed and 1,221 seriously injured. Excluding small numbers in north Wales, the statistics were as follows:

	Dead	**Seriously injured**
Swansea	387	412
Cardiff	355	502
Newport	51	63
Elsewhere in Glamorgan	32	120
Pembrokeshire	45	42
Monmouthshire (excl. Newport)	25	36
Carmarthenshire	14	13

Moreover, Swansea suffered greater material damage than anywhere else in Wales. Taking the two other large towns which were bombed, one can see that in twenty-three raids on Cardiff, between 500 and 600 properties were destroyed and 29,998 damaged, while in Newport, 4,533 buildings were damaged.[16]

Swansea's experience showed that it was perhaps erroneous to regard tonnage of high explosives as the yardstick by which to measure the intensity of a raid. In the case of Swansea (and, indeed, many other British towns) it was the fires caused by incendiary bombs which inflicted the most severe damage. This was particularly true of the 'Three Nights' Blitz', especially on the third night.

NOTES

1. For a general contemporary overview, see *The Second Industrial Survey of South Wales* (3 vols., Cardiff, 1937).
2. N. Arthur, *Swansea at War* (Manchester, 1988), pp. 4–7, 62–82; D. Boorman, 'The Port and its Worldwide Trade', *Swansea. An Illustrated History*, ed. Glanmor Williams (Swansea, 1990), pp. 79–80.
3. D. Trevor Williams, *The Economic Development of Swansea and of the Swansea District to 1921* (Cardiff, 1940), *passim*.
4. P.R. Reynolds, 'Industrial Development', *Swansea. An Illustrated History*, ed.Williams, pp. 52–5; T. Boyns, 'Industrialisation', *The City of Swansea. Challenges and Change*, ed. R. A. Griffiths (Stroud, 1990), pp. 46–9.
5. J.R. Alban, 'Preparations for Air Raid Precautions in Swansea', *Morgannwg*, xxviii (1984), 57–9; Arthur, *op. cit.*, p. 4.
6. K. Wakefield, *The First Pathfinders. The Operational History of Kampfgruppe 100, 1939–41* (repr. Somerton, 1992), p. 220.
7. Alban, *op. cit.*, pp. 68–9.

8. See also J.R. Alban, *Air Raids on Swansea* (Swansea, 1981); K. Pryer, *Luftwaffe over Swansea* (Swansea, n.d.), pp. 10–20; Arthur, *op. cit.*, pp. 34–5. The descriptions of the attacks given in this chapter are principally based on these works. Alban, *Air Raids* is a resources pack, thus references to it in this book will not contain page numbers.
9. *Völkischer Beobachter*, 18 February 1943.
10. *Hitler's War Directives, 1939–45*, ed. H.R. Trevor-Roper (London, 1964), pp. 56–9.
11. ibid., pp. 102–4.
12. *Kriegstagebuch des Oberkommandos der Wehrmacht*, pp. 1000–1. I am grateful to Professor Rhys W. Williams for drawing this reference to my attention.
13. W. Murray, *Luftwaffe. Strategy for Defeat, 1933–45* (London, 1985), pp. 25, 29–30.
14. B. Collier, *The Defence of the United Kingdom* (London, 1957), pp. 266, 272.
15. ibid., p. 504.
16. *SWEP*, 24 October 1944.

CHAPTER 2

The 'Three Nights' Blitz'

Considered collectively, the 'Three Nights' Blitz' was for Swansea the most severe raid of the war, and came at a time when the town was still licking its wounds after the fairly heavy blitz of 17 January 1941. The attack came on a town which was not unprepared for it, yet which still felt the shock. The contemporary reports printed in this edition will collectively give details of the attacks on each of the three nights. The following account is merely an outline of the events which occurred.

At 7.23 p.m. on the evening of Wednesday, 19 February 1941, the ARP authorities in Swansea received their first warning of the approach of a force of hostile aircraft. At that point in time it was uncertain whether the enemy's target was to be Swansea itself, as there had been many previous instances when the authorities had stood on the alert only to discover that the raiders had passed on, to attack targets elsewhere. However, warning 'red', the signal which meant 'raiders imminent', was given at 7.37 p.m., and the town was in no doubt that it was indeed to be the target, as two minutes later Heinkel 111s of *III. Kampfgeschwader 27* began their attack by dropping parachute flares and a combination of high explosive bombs. At 8.02 p.m., *Kampfgruppe 100*, the elite 'pathfinder force' arrived over the target and dropped a large mixture of incendiary bombs which caused fires at which the units following were able to release their loads of high explosive bombs and incendiaries. In all, sixty-one attacking aircraft dropped a total of 49.2 tonnes of high explosive (consisting of 442 bombs) and 15,720 incendiary bombs in a raid which ended when the last aircraft of K.G. 1 broke off at 11.03 p.m. The authorities, however, stayed on alert until the 'all clear' was given at 11.59 p.m., and then, for the rest of the night, the ARP services were involved with fire-fighting and rescue work, tasks which continued for the whole of the following day. If contemporary British accounts are to be believed, the

Figure 5. Fires rage in central Swansea on 21 February 1941. The only known photograph of the 'Three Nights' Blitz' in progress. *SAO.*

defensive forces coped successfully with the incendiary bombs, although high explosive bombs did do a lot of damage.

On the following night, the preliminary warning was received at 7.40 p.m. and warning 'red' eight minutes later. The first wave of bombers, Heinkel 111s of the II./ K.G. 27, began their attack at 8.00 p.m. with flares and high explosive bombs, many of which were delayed action devices. At 8.02 p.m., the pathfinder unit, K.Gr.100 arrived, with a huge consignment of 12,672 incendiaries. The fires caused by K.Gr. 100's incendiaries were then themselves the targets of the varied mixture of high explosive bombs dropped by *Gruppen* of the K.G. 26, K.G. 27, and K.G. 76. Then at 9.50 p.m. a further 4,032 incendiaries were dropped, together with a heavy load of high explosive bombs, by K.G. 1. Finally, two *Gruppen* of K.G. 77 completed the raid with a load of high explosive and incendiaries, breaking off at 11.45 p.m.

The raid of the 20th, coming as it did so close on the heels of the previous night's attack stretched the defence services to capacity, their efforts being hampered by the large number of delayed action bombs which had been dropped and by the number of craters and fallen buildings which cut off access to many parts of the central town. The raid had been even heavier than the previous night's, with 58.4 tonnes of high explosive bombs (a total of 404 bombs) and 19,944 incendiary bombs being dropped in a period which lasted nearly four hours. A short time after the attack began, the ARP Controller was obliged to summon mutual aid from rescue services from Llanelli, Neath, and Port Talbot. Fire engines and other rescue vehicles queued up at Llansamlet ready to be directed to those parts of the town where they were needed. Although the 'all clear' was sounded at 12.24 a.m., this brought no respite to the ARP personnel, who worked all through the night and all the following day combating the ravages of the attack.

On the final night, the 'raiders imminent' warning was given at 7.30 p.m. and the attack began at 7.50 p.m. The pattern of this raid was slightly different from the others. The first three waves of attackers dropped 339 high explosive bombs of varying sizes and types, presumably with the intention of further softening up an already fragile target. Then at 8.28 p.m. came the first wave of incendiary bombs, when K.Gr.100 released 13,824

Figure 6. Fighting the fires in Ben Evans's department store, from Wind Street. *SAO.*

of them over the town centre, with devastating effect. These were followed by a further three waves of aircraft from K.Gr. 606, K.G. 1, and II./ K.G. 26, which dropped a mixture of high explosives and incendiaries. The effects on the ARP services on the ground were devastating. As bad as the fires had been on the first two nights, they were nothing in comparison to those of the third night. In a period of four hours, an enormous total of 20,436 incendiary bombs rained down on the middle of Swansea causing fires which were exacerbated by gas mains fractured by high explosive bombs, while the damage to water mains by the same explosions hampered fire fighting. In addition, the large number of unexploded bombs in the town centre made the position of the defenders even more precarious. Eye witness accounts described the miles of hose pipes snaking through the town, many of them impotent through having been severed by explosions.[1] Indeed, on the third night the water mains were so badly damaged that supplies had to be piped from the North and South Docks. The fires, raging out of control, caused a glow which could be seen from as far afield as Pembrokeshire and Devon. In this raid, a total of 429 high explosive bombs adding up to 47.6 tonnes fell on Swansea, but it was the incendiaries which

Figure 7. Royal Engineers bomb disposal team at YMCA canteen in High Street. *SAO.*

did the greatest damage. The last bombers withdrew at midnight, although the 'all clear' did not sound until 12.40 a.m.

The following morning fires were still raging in the town centre, but, despite the apprehension, the raiders did not return that night, nor were there to be further attacks until early March. This lull gave Swansea time to take stock of its situation. The report of the ARP Controller and other official records sum the situation up.

It was clear even by the day following the last raid that three nights of attacks had been disastrous. The death toll stood at 122 men, sixty-eight women, and thirty-seven children under the age of sixteen. In addition, 254 persons had been seriously hurt and 137 slightly injured. By the standards of cities such as Coventry, the casualty list was relatively slight. However, in material terms, the town had suffered heavily. Forty-one acres of the centre were reduced to rubble, 282 houses and 575 business premises were totally destroyed, and 11,084 properties were damaged in some way. The enormous problems which were encountered by the ARP authorities and

Figure 8. Damaged houses in Teilo Crescent, Mayhill. *SAO.*

the details of the damage and immediate aftermath are summed up in the report made by the ARP Controller to the Council on 18 March 1941, which is printed in full below. Although it was classed as 'private and confidential', the report does not, however, give precise details of the totals of properties damaged or destroyed, or the number of casualties sustained. In fact, the casualty figures were not released until October 1944,[2] by which time their relative lowness was not believed by the majority of the inhabitants of Swansea. People could see the enormous amount of damage around them and had concluded that the casualties must have numbered thousands.

The documents published in this edition give details of the raids and their immediate aftermath, but do not reveal just how long afterwards the effects of the 'Three Nights' Blitz' continued to be felt in Swansea and its surrounding area. In the months following the attacks the ARP authorities had enormous logistical burdens in organizing billets and compensation for the homeless, the removal of dangerous buildings, the establishment of alternative shopping outlets, and many other necessary activities.[3] With

Figure 9. College Street and Gower Street, looking west. *SAO.*

much of the town centre reduced to a mass of rubble, many retailers and businesses were obliged to seek long-term accommodation elsewhere, and many of them found it in Mansel Street and Walter Road, former residential thoroughfares on the periphery of the central town area. While many firms returned to the town centre after the war, Mansel Street and Walter Road have remained to this day primarily as a business area, housing solicitors' and estate agents' offices. By the same token, before the blitz many people had lived in the town centre, but with post-war rebuilding, it lost its residential character, being redeveloped almost exclusively as a commercial centre.

Only in late 1942 was the first serious thought given to reconstructing the town centre, when the Borough Engineer was instructed to draft preliminary proposals for works to take place after cessation of hostilities. Of course, while the war progressed, these could only be ideas, but the first concept which emerged was for a 'processional way' which would link the town centre with the Guildhall. Scale models were actually built, but the plan never came to fruition since it would have necessitated the acquisition

Figure 10. Castle Street and College Street junction, looking south. *SAO.*

Figure 11. Aerial view showing the extent of damage in central Swansea. *SAO.*

and demolition of more properties than had actually been blitzed! In fact, the blitz of February 1943 temporarily halted thinking about post-war reconstruction, although by the end of the year more ideas were on the drawing board.

Eventually, a plan for a shopping precinct was adopted and the first compulsory purchase orders were issued in 1946 under the terms of the Planning Act, 1944. By the end of the 1940s, many bombed sites in the centre had been cleared, and twenty-seven temporary Nissen hut shops had been erected. Several new roads were laid, the first, the Kingsway, being opened in November 1950. Reconstruction continued into the 1950s, with numerous rectangular, functional 'shoe-box' buildings being erected, their appearance being in stark contrast to the more grandiose and ornate Victorian and Edwardian buildings which had graced the town centre before the blitz. But reconstruction took time: the sheer extent of the work, coupled initially with shortage of building materials, meant that redevelopment took place throughout the fifties and into the sixties.

St Mary's parish church, for example, did not reopen for worship until 1959;[4] the late Victorian Oxford Street Market, which had been gutted by incendiaries, losing its huge two-acre roof of glass and wrought iron, was not rebuilt until 1961.[5] In fact, the full redevelopment was not completed until the building of the Quadrant Centre in the late 1970s, by which time attention was being given to upgrading areas adjacent to those which had been blitzed, including the redundant former South Dock and the Maritime Quarter, and this work continues into the 1990s.

The most lasting result of the 'Three Nights' Blitz' was the disappearance of the old town centre, the one with its distinctive buildings such as Ben Evans's department store, and its narrow streets, which featured in the reminiscences of Dylan Thomas. In many respects, the face of central Swansea today is a reminder of the German air raids, and especially those of February 1941.

NOTES

1. *Western Mail, Bombers over Wales* (Cardiff, n.d.), pp. 14–16; Alban, *Air Raids on Swansea.* For some eyewitness accounts, see Aneirin ap Talfan, *Dyddiau'r Ceiliog Rhedyn. Abertawe, Ionawr-Chwefror, 1941* (Llundain, n.d. [1943]) (English translation, 'Days of the Grasshopper. Swansea, January–February 1941', by Alan Rees, in SCA, FAC 151); SCA, D.35: war-time diaries of Laurie Latchford; WGRO, D/D Z 126: diary of Will Thomas, air raid warden, St Thomas, August 1940 – September 1941.
2. *SWEP*, 24 October 1944.
3. J.R. Alban, 'The Second World War', *The City of Swansea. Challenges and Change,* ed. R.A. Griffiths (Stroud, 1990), pp. 132–3.
4. D.G. Walker, *St Mary's Church, Swansea* (3rd. edn., Swansea, 1967), pp. 32–44.
5. J.R. Alban, *Markets in Swansea* (Swansea, 1991), pp. 12–15.

CHAPTER 3

The Organization of Civil Defence in Swansea

At the time of the 'Three Nights' Blitz', the civil defence of Swansea was in the hands of the local authority, the County Borough of Swansea.[1] However, in common with many other British towns, the first precautionary measures against possible future air raids were set in train in 1935, long before the actual outbreak of war. Since the end of the First World War, the British government had been aware of the potential threat which the bomber might hold in any future war, and from at least 1924 onwards, the Air Raid Precautions Sub-Committee of the Committee of Imperial Defence had been involved in a serious study of the possible dangers. The worsening international situation in the 1930s led the government to take positive measures, thus in July 1935, it issued the 'First Circular on Air Raid Precautions'. This invited local authorities to cooperate voluntarily with local employers in drafting ARP schemes for their localities. Since the proposals of the circular were not obligatory in law, the response to it throughout the country was lukewarm. Swansea did, however, avail itself of anti-gas training for its police force, fire brigade, and for many members of Guildhall staff, while representatives were sent to a regional conference on ARP held at Cardiff.

The relative ineffectiveness of the 'First Circular' spurred the government on to more positive steps, and in November 1937, an Air Raid Precautions Act was passed, coming into force on 1 January 1938. This act imposed upon local authorities the legal obligation to take precautions for the 'protection of persons and property from injury or damage in the event of hostile attack from the air'. Swansea's response to the act was immediate, and in February 1938, the first meeting of the County Borough's ARP Committee took place, under the chairmanship of

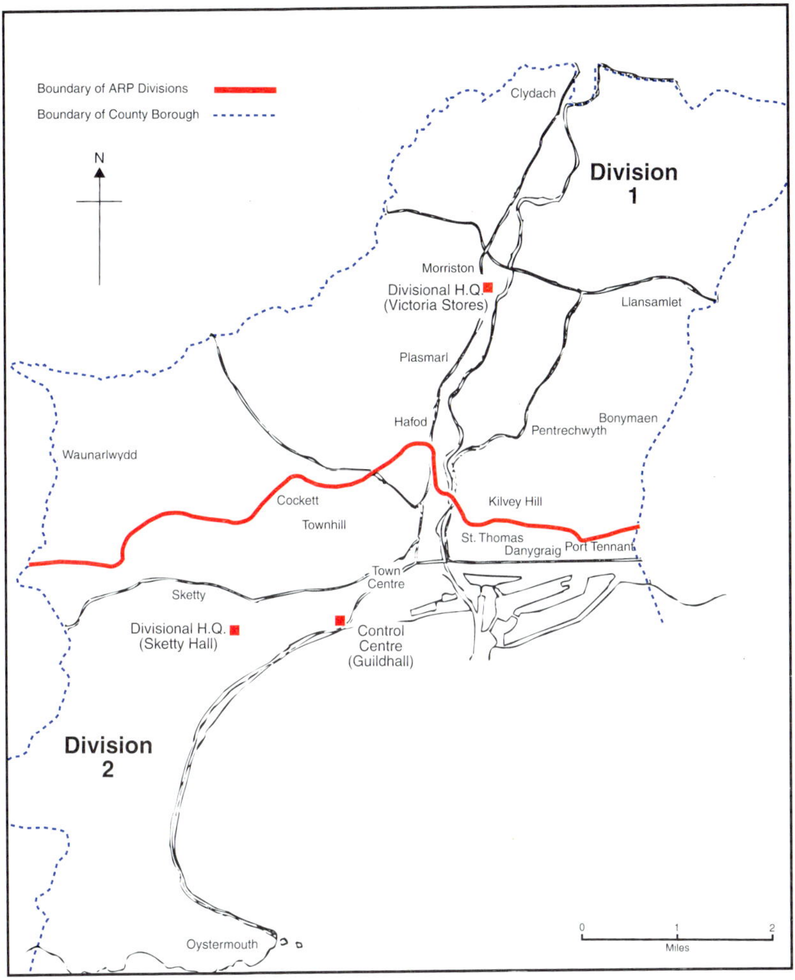

Figure 12. ARP Divisions after March 1939.

Alderman Percy Morris, who was to play a major role in civil defence, both in Swansea and south Wales.

1938 and 1939 saw great activity in Swansea, as ARP measures were put into place, and after the declaration of war, these measures increased in intensity. In May 1938, the first ARP Officer was appointed, with a brief to establish an ARP Department responsible to the Town Clerk, who, in April 1939, was designated ARP Controller for the County Borough, with the responsibility, in war time, for the coordination of the various ARP and other services whenever attacks occurred. The two years leading up to the war saw a massive recruitment drive for personnel to serve in the various branches of ARP, as wardens, ambulance drivers, in rescue parties or first aid parties, and so on. Defensive measures included the provision and testing of warning sirens, supplying of gas masks, sandbags, and domestic shelters, the construction of public shelters and static water tanks for fire-fighting, and the acquisition of premises to serve a variety of needs, including first aid centres, ambulance depots, garages, stores, and mortuaries.

Many steps were taken for countering the ravages of attacks and for dealing with their aftermath. Mutual aid arrangements were made with neighbouring authorities and fire services, and, within Swansea itself, with employers and voluntary organizations such as the Red Cross, St John's Ambulance Brigade, the Women's Voluntary Service, and the Boy Scout movement. By the outbreak of war, the preparations for civil defence were more or less complete. The ARP Department had established in Swansea a comprehensive network of air raid wardens, an Auxiliary Fire Service, an ambulance service, first aid parties, rescue parties, demolition parties and other units necessary to deal with raids and their aftermath, working in close conjunction with the Borough Police Force and the police fire brigade.

In the late 1930s, one of the major realizations was that air raids in any future war would almost certainly be accompanied by fires. Before the war, the County Borough of Swansea had had an efficient, modern fire brigade controlled and manned by the Borough Police Force. Thus the Fire Brigades Act, 1938, which was aimed at improving substandard fire-fighting arrangements, had little bearing on Swansea. However, under the Air Raid Precautions Act of the same year, the County Borough of Swansea was obliged to provide an Auxiliary Fire Service as part of its general measures for ARP within its administrative area. In April 1938, the first steps to recruit and train a force of 500 auxiliary firemen and support staff were put in hand, and construction also began of a series of emergency water tanks, so that by the end of 1941, there were forty-six of them in the borough. The auxiliary force, with its administrative headquarters in Northampton Gardens, was made up of two divisions, 'A' and 'B'. The former, with its divisional headquarters in St Thomas, covered the town centre, the east side and northern Swansea, the latter, with its headquarters in Sketty, covered the western side of the town. Each division was divided into sections, each with its sectional station, while the districts covered by the sectional stations were split up into patrol areas, which themselves were further divided into beats. Within the patrol areas, there were a number of designated 'action stations', usually based in shops or garages which had telephones. The force consisted of both full-time and part-time personnel, and its main role was to provide support for the regular Swansea Police Fire Brigade. Like the police force it came within the remit of the Borough Watch Committee and was under the command of the Chief Constable.

Figure 13. AFS officers at a Canadian mobile canteen outside the Guildhall. *SAO.*

A sophisticated system for the general control of ARP had been established in Swansea by March 1939. The main air raid control room, from which the ARP Controller and his staff directed operations during an emergency, was housed in the Green Room at the Guildhall. The County Borough itself was organized into two divisions, each under the control of a Divisional Warden. Division 1 had its headquarters in the Victoria Stores in Morriston, and covered the area of the town roughly to the north of the Great Western Railway line which ran eastwards from Cockett to the Landore viaduct. At the Landore viaduct, the boundary veered south towards Foxhole, then skirted the southern face of Kilvey Hill above Grenfell Park and St Thomas. Division 2 , with its headquarters in Sketty Hall, took in the town centre, Danygraig, Port Tennant, and St Thomas to the east of the river Tawe, and the western parts of the borough south of the GWR railway line.

Each Division was itself subdivided into Groups, the boundaries of which were more or less coterminous with those of the electoral wards. Each group was identified by a letter of the alphabet, and was under the control of a Group Warden. The Groups were further split up into Sectors, the precise number of which varied in relation to the density of population within the Group, central town Groups having more Sectors than suburban Groups. The Sectors, which were identified by numbers, were each under the command of a Sector Warden, who had control of all wardens and wardens' posts within his Sector.

This was the civil defence machinery which came into action to combat enemy air attacks on Swansea, including those of the 'Three Nights' Blitz'. Although the raids of those three nights clearly stretched these resources to their limit, the ARP services' efficiency and high levels of organization, which had been born of pre-war planning, helped to minimize the worst effects of the raids, particularly with regard to casualties, as later government assessments clearly pointed out.

In addition to the 'passive' defence force of the ARP organization, Swansea also had a series of more active defences. Key installations, such as the docks and some factories, were protected by a barrage of balloons. These were the responsibility of the Royal Air Force and the local squadron, no. 958, was a unit of no. 14 Balloon Centre, Cardiff, which ultimately came under the command of no. 32 (Barrage Balloon) Group, whose group headquarters was at Romsey.[2] In the early months of 1941, there were thirty-five balloons in the Swansea area, three of which were waterborne. The German raid reports record the barrage balloons around Swansea as being at an altitude of between 1,600 and 2,000 metres.

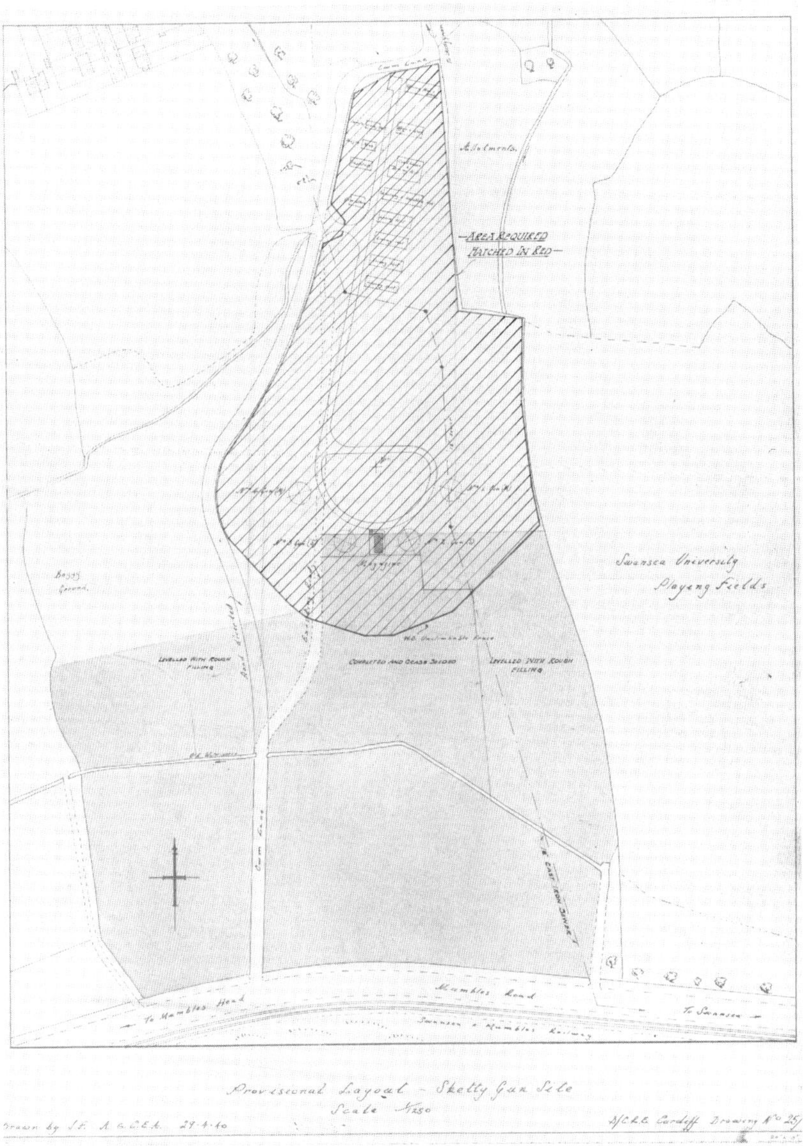

Figure 14. Layout of Gun Site 'T' at King George V Playing Fields. *SAO.*

Swansea was also defended by anti-aircraft batteries under the control of the 5th Anti-Aircraft Division, who also operated searchlights. Twenty-four heavy anti-aircraft guns were housed in emplacements at Winch Wen, Mumbles, Ravenhill, and other sites. Although in his report the ARP Controller stated that Swansea was below its quota of anti-aircraft guns, by the time of the attacks of February 1941, the town was reasonably well protected by barrage balloons, guns, and searchlights. However, while the levels of provision may not have been perfect, they were a far cry from the state of affairs of the previous summer. When the first raids occurred, Swansea had no anti-aircraft guns (although Cardiff had twelve and Newport, four), and there were only sixteen barrage balloons in the whole of Glamorgan. Indeed, one official report dating from June 1940 described Wales as being 'defenceless'. However, by July, sixteen heavy anti-aircraft guns had made their appearance in Swansea. Nevertheless, complaints about their inadequacies were officially voiced after the raids of August and by early September the deficiency had been largely rectified, one contemporary diarist commenting at the end of that month on the 'terrific rate of fire' of the new weapons.[3]

The anti-aircraft guns were not greatly effective in bringing down enemy aircraft, but they did help to keep them flying high, thereby reducing the accuracy of their bombing, and they did, through their noise, assist in boosting civilian morale. (Indeed, during the 'Three Nights' Blitz', naval guns at Mumbles Head were also fired to add to the noise.) However, when the anti-aircraft guns stopped firing on the night of 21 February (because nightfighters were operating in the area and because the control centre had been temporarily knocked out of action by a bomb) there was great public concern and outcry in Swansea, which the authorities went to great lengths to appease.

In terms of fighter cover, Swansea, at the time of the 'Three Nights' Blitz', lay within the Pembrey Sector of RAF Fighter Command's 10 Group, whose Group Headquarters was at Box in Wiltshire. (The fighter base at Fairwood Common did not become operational until June 1941, and it became a Sector Station in its own right in the following October.)[4] Units of *Luftflotten 2* and *3*, on their way to bomb Swansea, also had to run the gauntlet of other 10 Group fighter squadrons based at airfields in the St Eval, Middle Wallop, and Filton Sectors in the west of England. The German raid reports refer to the activity of one nightfighter over the target and two over the Bristol Channel on 19 February, while on 21 February, two nightfighters were encountered over Swansea and one over the English Channel near Start Point in Devonshire. The German reference to the two nightfighters over the target on the last night of the raids confirms the explanation given by the British authorities as to why the anti-aircraft guns stopped firing.

NOTES

1. For a fuller discussion and background to the subject matter of this chapter, see J.R. Alban, 'Preparations for Air Raid Precautions in Swansea, 1935–9', *Morgannwg*, xxviii (1984), 55–73.
2. B. Collier, *The Defence of the United Kingdom*, pp. 445–7; N. Arthur, *Swansea at War*, pp. 11–15.
3. Collier, *op. cit.*, pp. 479–81; Arthur, *op. cit.*, p. 11; SCA, D.35: Diary of Laurie Latchford, entry for 13 September 1940. Extracts from the war-time diairies of Laurie Latchford, an ARP warden in Swansea, were also published as 'Swansea at War: a Civilian Diary' in *SWEP* (2–20 September 1980).
4. Collier, *op. cit.*, pp. 442–4, 453–5; Arthur, *op. cit.*, pp. 107–8.

Figure 15. ARP workers in the ruins of David Evans's store. *SAO.*

CHAPTER 4

Luftwaffe Units involved in the 'Three Nights' Blitz'

The bombers which attacked Swansea in February 1941 were exclusively from units of the airfleets *Luftflotte 2* and *Luftflotte 3*, based in northern and western France. At the time of the 'Three Nights' Blitz' there were five *Luftflotten. Luftflotten 1* and *4* were home based and respectively covered north-east and south-west Germany. Attacks on the United Kingdom were mainly carried out by *Luftflotten 2* and *3*, with *Luftflotte 5*, based in Norway and Denmark, undertaking attacks on shipping in the North Sea and on Scotland and the north-east of England. Shortly afterwards, a *Luftflotte 6* was established for operations in central Russia. Each of the *Luftflotten* was a self-contained air force, with its own fighter, bomber, reconnaissance, *Zerstörer*, *Stuka*, training, and other units.[1]

In February 1941, *Luftflotte 2*, under the command of *Generalfeldmarschall* Albert Kesselring, was based at airfields in the Netherlands, Belgium, and part of northern France, with its headquarters in Brussels. The units of *Luftflotte 2* which bombed Swansea were all based in France, at airfields in an area north of the boundary between it and the region controlled by *Luftflotte 3*, a line which ran from the mouth of the river Seine, close by the north of Paris, and on through the Belgian border.

Luftflotte 3, with its headquarters in Paris, was under the command of *Generalfeldmarschall* Hugo Sperrle, and its main airfields for offences against the United Kingdom were in the western part of France, in Normandy and Brittany. In 1940, each of these airfleets had been allocated an area of Britain for its attacks, *Luftflotte 2* to the east of the country, and *Luftflotte 3* to the west. However, in the course of the Battle of Britain, such a geographical distinction became blurred and then disappeared, so that

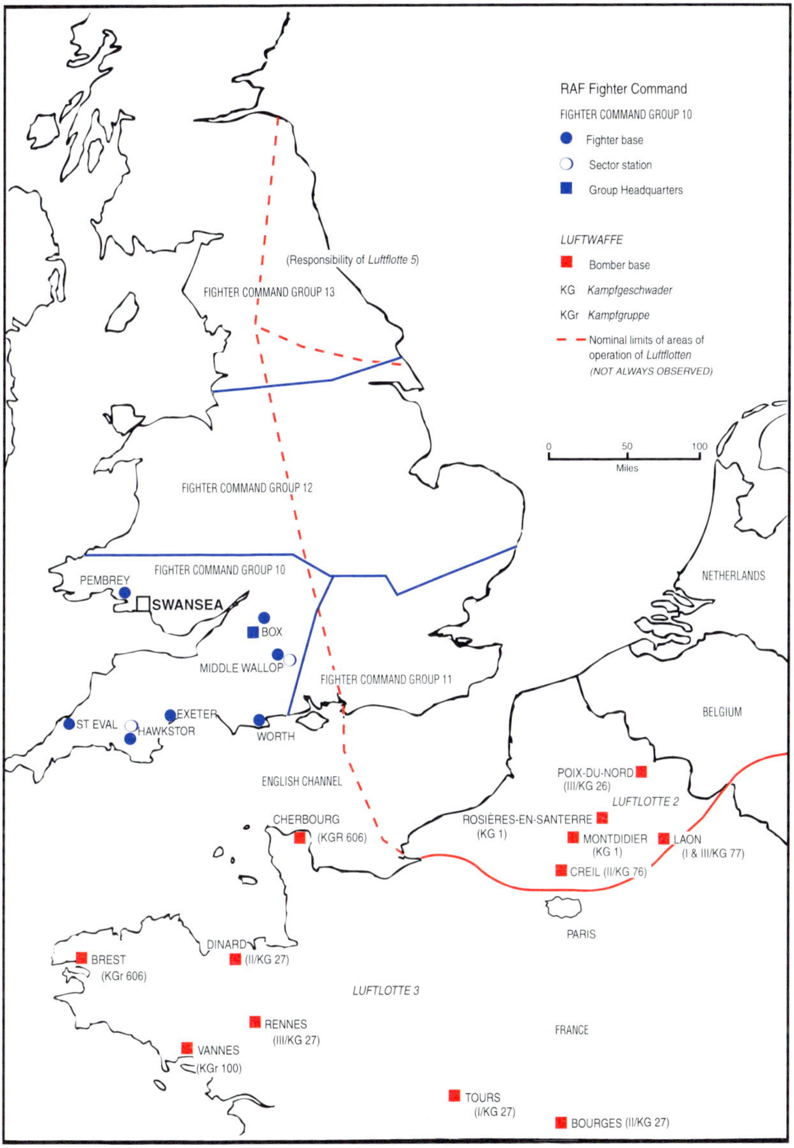

Figure 16. Bases of *Luftwaffe* units involved in the 'Three Nights' Blitz'.

units of *Luftflotte 2*, for example, were employed in the raids of February 1941 on Swansea.

For administrative purposes, each *Luftflotte* area was subdivided into air zones known as *Luftgaue*, the personnel of which were responsible for logistical and technical support. The parallel subdivision for operational purposes was the *Fliegerkorps*, which was responsible for operating between 300 and 750 aircraft. The *Fliegerkorps* was usually subordinated to the *Luftflotte* within whose area it lay.

The smallest operational unit, whether of fighters, bombers, or other aircraft, was the *Staffel*, which, commanded by a *Staffelkapitän* (usually an *Oberleutnant* or *Hauptmann*), comprised nine aircraft. Three *Staffeln* and a headquarters flight known as a *Stab* made up a *Gruppe*, under the command of a *Kommandeur* (usually a *Hauptmann* or *Major*). The *Gruppe* usually occupied one airfield, and its *Kommandeur* would usually be assisted by an adjutant, a medical officer, and technical officers.

Three *Gruppen*, with a total of about ninety aircraft, made up a *Geschwader*, which, additionally, was complemented with a *Stab* flight of a further four aircraft. The officer commanding a *Geschwader* was designated *Kommodore* and usually held the rank of *Major, Oberstleutnant,* or *Oberst*, and had under him a comprehensive staff of adjutant, operations officer, signals officer, navigational officer, technical officers, and other specialists.

The units described above were further identified by a suffix which explained their precise role. A fighter *Geschwader*, for example, would be known as *Jagdgeschwader*, a dive bomber unit as *Stukageschwader*. The main bomber unit was called the *Kampfgeschwader*, made up of *Kampfgruppen*, although for certain specialist roles such as that of pathfinder units, independent *Kampfgruppen* were set up. All *Kampfgeschwäder* and specialist independent *Kampfgruppen* were numbered with Arabic numerals, thus *Kampfgeschwader 27*, or *Kampfgruppe 100*. Those *Gruppen* which formed part of a *Geschwader*, however, were differentiated by Roman numerals, hence I./K.G. 77 indicated the first *Gruppe* of *Kampfgeschwader 77*, II./K.G. 26, the second *Gruppe* of *Kampfgeschwader 26*. The first three *Staffeln* in a *Geschwader* formed the first *Gruppe*, *Staffeln 4*, *5*, and *6* the second *Gruppe*, and *Staffeln 7*, *8*, and *9* the third *Gruppe*.

The units which attacked Swansea on the nights of 19, 20, and 21 February 1941 were all based at airfields in western or northern France, bases which had come into the Germans' hands when that country fell to them in the early summer of 1940.[2] The airfields nearest to Swansea were those belonging to *Luftflotte 3*, and lying in Brittany and in the Cotentin peninsula of Normandy, or further south near the Loire. *Kampfgeschwader 27*, equipped with Heinkel He. 111s, had three *Gruppen* which flew against Swansea on each of the three nights. The first *Gruppe* was based a fair distance inland at Tours, the second was split between Dinard near the Breton coast and at Bourges, which was south of the Loire, while the third was based at Rennes. The pathfinder force, *Kampfgruppe 100*, which flew He. 111s, was stationed at Vannes in Brittany, while the Dornier Do. 17s of *Kampfgruppe 606* were split between airfields at Brest and Cherbourg.

The aircraft of *Luftflotte 2* which were involved in the attacks on Swansea all came from bases to the north of Paris. *Kampfgeschwader 1*, with its He. 111s and Junkers Ju. 88s, was based at Montdidier and Rosières-en-Santerre. The He. 111s of *III. Kampfgeschwader 26* were based at Poix-du-Nord near Amiens, while the Ju. 88s of *II. Kampfgeschwader 76* were at Creil and those of *I.* and *III. Kampfgeschwader 77* were at Laon. All these bases, both of *Luftflotte 2* and *Luftflotte 3*, were well within striking distance of Swansea, although most of the units involved in the attacks had to cross the English South Coast or the South-West Peninsula to actually reach their destination. In so doing, they ran the risk of encountering flak and night fighter activity even before they arrived at target. Such problems are clearly mentioned in the German reports.

Units which Participated in the 'Three Nights' Blitz'

Luft-flotte	**Unit**	**Base**	**Identification Markings**	**Aircraft Type**
3	I./K.G.27	Tours	1G	He. 111s
3	II./K.G.27	Dinard & Bourges	1G	He. 111s
3	III./K.G.27	Rennes	1G	He. 111s
3	K.Gr.100	Vannes	6N	He. 111s
3	K.Gr.606	Brest & Cherbourg	7T	Do. 17s
2	K.G.1	Montdidier & Rosières-en-Santerre	V4	He. 111s & Ju. 88s
2	III./K.G.26	Poix-du-Nord	1H	He. 111s
2	II./K.G.76	Creil	F1	Ju. 88s
2	I./K.G.77	Laon	3Z	Ju. 88s
2	III./K.G.77	Laon	3Z	Ju. 88s

NOTES

1. The description of *Luftwaffe* organization is based upon the following works: A. Price, *Luftwaffe Handbook, 1939–45* (London, 1977); L. Deighton and M. Hastings, *Battle of Britain* (London, 1980); F.K. Mason, *Battle over Britain* (London, 1969); and A. Ward, *A Nation Alone. The Battle of Britain*, 1940 (London, 1989).

2. Information on *Luftwaffe* units is based on Deighton and Hastings, *op. cit.*, B. Collier, *The Defence of the United Kingdom*, pp.463–7, and K. Wakefield, *The First Pathfinders* (repr. Somerton, 1992).

CHAPTER 5

German Aircraft involved in the 'Three Nights' Blitz'

Three types of aircraft were used by the *Luftwaffe* units which bombed Swansea on 19, 20, and 21 February 1941. All were twin-engined, medium bombers, which had been developed during the 1930s and which, with one exception, the Ju. 88, were not really successful in terms of range, bomb loads carried, or armament.[1]

By far the most heavily involved bomber in the 'Three Nights' Blitz' was the Heinkel He. 111. This is not surprising, as in 1941, the He.111 equipped about three-quarters of the *Luftwaffe's* twin-engined bomber units. This aircraft had originally been introduced as an airliner in the 1930s, but had undergone secret tests as a bomber. Its early marques saw service in the Spanish Civil War, while it also flew covert photographic reconnaissance missions over the United Kingdom, France, and the Soviet Union in 1937, disguised in Lufthansa civil airline markings. The He. 111 had a cigar shaped fuselage, with a heavily glazed nose. This afforded excellent all round forward vision, but made the crew feel very vulnerable.

With its bombs held nose upright within its bomb bays, the He. 111 could carry a bomb load of 4,400 lbs., which was almost twice that of the Dornier Do. 17 and 1,000 lbs. more than the Junkers Ju. 88. Of the three mainline bombers it could thus certainly deliver the largest payload. Its range was 745 miles, with an operational ceiling of 25,590 feet. However, it had many drawbacks. In common with the Do. 17 and the Ju. 88, the crew of four or five were closely cramped together in the forward part of the fuselage, making them all vulnerable if the aircraft were attacked. Moreover, the aircraft was relatively under powered, with a top speed of 247 miles per hour. Its heavy armour assisted in slowing it down, although it also meant that the He. 111 was a tough workhorse. The aircraft's defensive armament, consisting of five hand-operated 7.9 mm. MG 15 machine guns, which were not easily brought to bear on fast moving interceptors, was not greatly effective, and by autumn 1940, the Heinkel bomber had been relegated to night actions.

In the raids of 19 and 21 February, *Kampfgruppe 606* flew Dornier Do. 17s. Known as 'the flying pencil', the Do. 17 first flew in 1934 as a prototype airliner and airmail carrier. Unsuccessful in these roles, it was developed as a *Schnellbomber* by the *Luftwaffe*, and saw service in the Spanish Civil War in a reconnaissance role. By 1941, however, it was obsolescent, although it still equipped just under a quarter of the *Luftwaffe's* bomber and reconnaissance units. Its crew of four were concentrated towards the front of a fuselage which carried less armour than the He. 111. The bomb load, of 2,200 lbs., was poor by the standards of 1941, as was the armament of between five and eight hand-held 7.9 mm. MG 15 machine guns. The Do. 17 was equipped with two BMW Bramo Fafnir 323P engines, each of 1,000 horsepower. Slightly faster than the He. 111, with a top speed of 265 mph, it had a range of 721 miles and an operational ceiling of 26,740 feet.

Figure 17. Heinkel He. 111s. *Barnaby's Picture Library.*

Figure 18. Dornier Do. 17. *Topham Picture Source.*

The Junkers Ju. 88 was a newer and far more versatile aircraft than either of the other two, although only a small number of this aircraft, belonging to *Kampfgeschwäder 1*, *76*, and *77*, took part in the 'Three Nights' Blitz' on Swansea. The Ju. 88 had first flown in 1936, and, since the aircraft was designed for dive bombing as well as horizontal bombing, it was therefore built to a far tougher specification than the He. 111 or the Do. 17. First entering production in 1939, it played a limited role during the Battle of Britain, where it proved, however, to be more than a match for British Blenheim and Defiant fighters. Indeed, later in the war, the Ju. 88 achieved spectacular success as a high altitude reconnaissance aircraft and especially

Figure 19. Junkers Ju. 88. *Barnaby's Picture Library.*

as a night fighter. At the time of the 'Three Nights' Blitz', the Ju. 88 was replacing He. 111s and Do. 17s in some units, *Kampfgeschwader 1*, with its mix of He. 111s and Ju. 88s, being a case in point.

The Ju. 88's four-man crew comprised pilot, bomb aimer/nose gunner, radio operator/rear gunner, and belly gunner, all of whom were housed in the forward section of the fuselage. The bomb load, of 3,300 lbs., was carried externally on pylons beneath the wings and near the fuselage or in two small internal bomb bays, while the armament consisted of three 7.9 mm. MG 15 machine guns, one in the nose, one at the rear of the cockpit canopy, and one in a ventral gondola. Powered by two Junkers Jumo 211 B-1 1,200 horsepower engines, the Ju. 88 was capable of 286 mph, and had a range of 1,453 miles, with a service ceiling of 26,500 feet.

The air campaign during the Battle of Britain in the autumn of 1940 had revealed the weaknesses of these aircraft against British single-engined fighters, particularly the Spitfire, during daytime operations, thus the general trend was to employ them only for night time raids or daylight attacks upon shipping. The 'Blitz' of early 1941 therefore consisted almost exclusively of night attacks, which brought with them the problems of accuracy in bombing and navigation.

In 1941, no air force possessed the skills and equipment for pin-point, accurate bombing at night, and this may in part explain the fairly wide territorial spread of the bombs which fell on Swansea and may also be one reason why the bulk of German raids on the town hit commercial and residential areas rather than the more obvious targets of industry and the docks. Another reason for lack of bombing accuracy was the relatively high altitudes from which the bombers made their attacks on Swansea. At targets which were protected by anti-aircraft defences, there was a tendency to fly high and in fairly loose formations for added protection. When over target, the bombers usually dropped their bombs individually, unless they had orders to undertake pattern bombing, in which case, the *Gruppe* leader would give the signal when ready. In the case of Swansea's 'Three Nights' Blitz', however, it appears that aircraft carried out their bombing runs individually, the units involved on each of the three nights approaching the town using the *'Krokodil'* tactics favoured by the *Luftwaffe* in its night raids during 1941. In this system, aircraft from the same unit flew along the same route at four-minute intervals and then bombed individually when they arrived over target. This is clearly seen in the German reports on

Swansea, and the result of this practice was that the activity of units over target was of fairly long duration, while the raids themselves could last many hours, as was certainly the case during the 'Three Nights' Blitz'.

In order to combat inaccuracy in navigation at night or in bad weather, the *Luftwaffe* employed radio aids in its aircraft. The most basic of these was the system code-named *Knickebein* ('bent leg'), which employed two 'Lorenz' radio beams.[2] The first beam was laid down as a guide to the target, and the pilot followed it by listening to a steady, unbroken tone emanating from the on-board receiver which was also used to pick up normal airfield approach signals. If he deviated to the left or right of the tracking beam, Morse code dots and dashes warned him of this. Over the target a second beam intersected the first and on receiving the second signal, the aircraft captain knew when to drop his bombs. This deceptively simple system, however, had its drawbacks: its accuracy was limited to 500 metres on either side of the tracking beam, and aircraft also had to fly at at least 20,000 feet to avoid losing the signal, while, once its existence was discovered by the British, it could be easily countered. There is no evidence to show that British counter measures were taken against the beams during Swansea's 'Three Nights' Blitz'.

Aircraft of the pathfinder units involved in the bombing of Swansea were equipped with more sophisticated apparatus which allowed for greater accuracy in target finding. Unlike *Knickebein*, which was fairly simple to use, these aids were more complicated and required specially equipped aircraft with crews trained in their use. *Kampfgruppe 100* used *X-Gerät*, a system which, like *Knickebein*, laid a tracking beam over the target, but then used a series of sensitive, intersecting beams, to warn the pilot that the target was imminent and to tell him when he was over target.[3] In so doing, the apparatus automatically prepared the bombs for release and then opened the bomb bay doors and dropped the bombs at the exact point above target. The *Y–Verfahren* used by thc other pathfinder unit, *III. Gruppe* of *Kampfgeschwader 26*, although similar in certain respects, was a slightly more sophisticated system. The German reports on the 'Three Nights' Blitz' refer to the majority of ordinary *Gruppen* as having bombed 'by sight of ground', whereas the pathfinder units always attacked 'using apparatus'.

NOTES

1. The information about German aircraft has been mainly extracted from the following works: *Jane's Fighting Aircraft of World War II* (London, 1990), pp. 160, 167, 171–3; L. Deighton and M. Hastings, *The Battle of Britain* (London, 1980, repr. 1990); K. Munson, *German Aircraft of World War Two* (London, 1978); A Price, *The Bomber in World War II* (London, 1976), pp. 80–90.
2. On the various bombing aids, see B. Johnson, *The Secret War* (London, 1978) and R.V. Jones, *Most Secret War* (London, 1978).
3. K. Wakefield, *The First Pathfinders* (repr. Somerton, 1992), pp. 20–7 and *passim;* A Price, *The Bomber in World War II*, pp. 70–3.

CHAPTER 6

German Bombs dropped on Swansea

The bombs dropped on Swansea during the 'Three Nights' Blitz' were of two main types: high explosive and incendiary.[1] Although in 1941 the Germans possessed bombs of a greater capacity, for instance, the SC 2500 *Max*, weighing 2,500 kilograms, or the *'Satan'*, of 2,000 kilograms, the largest high explosive device which fell on Swansea during the three raids was the 1,000 kilogram bomb, the smallest, the 50 kilogram bomb. There were two main types of high explosive bomb, differentiated by the thickness of their casings, and identified by a mnemonic prefix. The prefix was followed by a number, which indicated the weight of the bomb in kilograms. The designation SC (*Spreng Cylindrisch*, 'explosive, cylindrical') referred to a high explosive bomb with a thin wall which provided for maximum blast effect. The SD bomb (*Spreng Dickenwand*, 'explosive, thick-walled') was a high explosive fragmentation bomb. The only SDs dropped on Swansea during the 'Three Nights' Blitz' were SD 50s, whereas the greater numbers of thin-walled bombs dropped included SC 1000s, SC 500s, SC 250s, and SC 50s. Such a preponderance of SCs of various sizes was typical of all the German air raids on British towns during the Blitz of 1941. A number of the high explosive bombs dropped during Swansea's 'Three Nights' Blitz' were equipped with delayed action fuses, to add to the problems and uncertainties felt by the civil defence personnel on the ground. Such bombs bore the suffix LZZ (*Lange Zeit Zunder*, 'long time fuse') and usually weighed 250 kilograms, hence the designation SC 250 LZZ. These bombs could be timed to explode after thirty-six hours or more, and had the potential for causing havoc. The devastating effects of such bombs are clearly seen in the incident of the deaths of three little boys, which occurred at lunch time on 20 February 1941, and which was reported in the *South Wales Evening Post* of 21 February.[2]

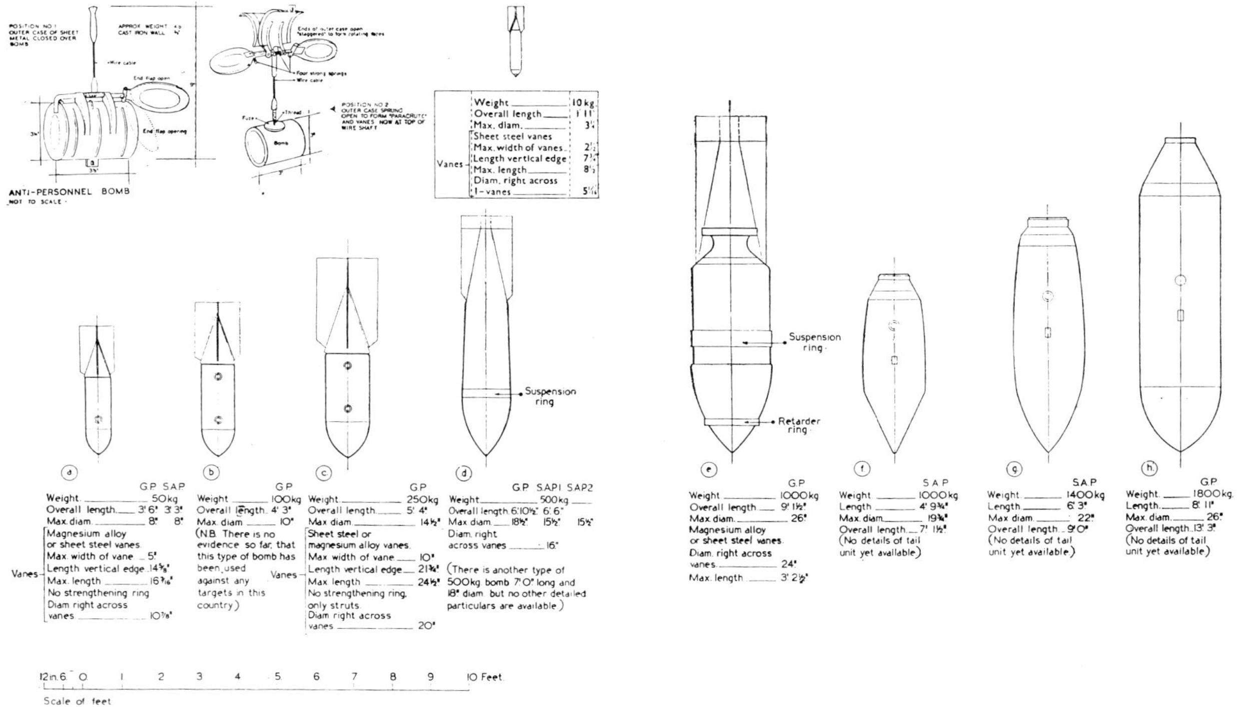

Figure 20. Types of German high explosive bombs from an ARP manual *Objects dropped from the Air* (London, 1941). *SAO.*

The two main types of incendiary bombs used in the raids were similar to one another in appearance. In fact, one was actually a derivative of the other. Both weighed 1 kilogram and had a casing made of combustible magnesium, with a tailfin of tinplate to assist aerodynamics. The basic, and more heavily used, type was the B1 El (*Brandbombe 1 Kilogram Elektron*), which ignited on contact. A more sophisticated version was the B1 El ZA, which contained a small explosive charge which detonated as the bomb was burning, throwing flaming debris over a radius of fifteen metres. This type of incendiary was capable of killing or seriously injuring anyone in its vicinity, or of spreading fire more rapidly than the B1 El. This was the type of bomb mentioned in the *South Wales Evening Post* report of 21 February as falling through the roof of a Swansea cinema on the first night of the 'Three Nights' Blitz'.

During the raids, the incendiaries were dropped in AB 36 canisters, each containing thirty-six bombs. In the German reports printed below, the incendiary loads carried by *I.* and *III. Gruppen* of *Kampfgeschwader 77* on the evening of 20/21 February were reckoned in terms of canisters rather than in individual bombs, unlike in the cases of all the other units which carried incendiary bombs on each of the three nights. After the canister was released from the aircraft, it broke apart when a clockwork mechanism, activated by an electro-magnet, raised a rod holding the ends of the canister together. The bombs then fell freely, scattering themselves over a fairly concentrated area and starting numerous fires. Because of their magnesium content, they were difficult to extinguish using a jet of water, and the most efficient means of putting them out was to smother them with sand or dry earth, although *sprinkled* water from a stirrup pump was also effective. Small through the incendiary bombs may have been in comparison to the high explosive bombs, it was the fires which they caused which resulted in the greatest damage within Swansea's town centre. Nevertheless, the high explosives had their role to play. The British reports indicate how the fire fighting services had, in fact, managed to control incendiary bomb fires on the first night of the raids. However, by the second, and particularly the third nights, when the defensive forces were extended to the limits of their endurance, the protracted effort and the damage to water and gas mains and to hose pipes caused by high explosives finally allowed the incendiary bomb fires to get out of control.

NOTES

1. On German bombs, see A. Price, *The Luftwaffe Handbook, 1939–45* (London, 1977), p. 41 and K. Wakefield, *The First Pathfinders*, pp. 239–40.

2. See pp. 137–8 below.

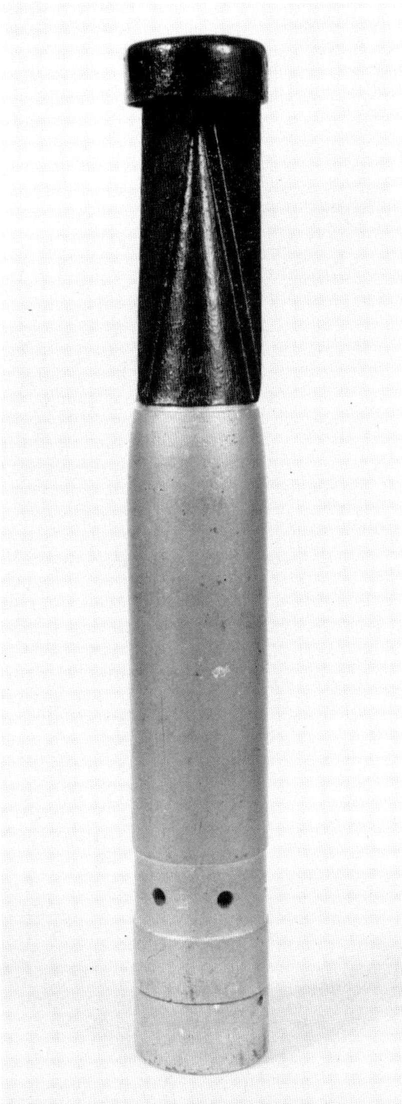

Figure 21. German incendiary bomb, type B1 E1 ZA, dropped on Swansea during the 'Three Nights' Blitz'. *SAO.*

Figure 22. German incendiary bomb container AB 36 which held thirty-six B1 E1 incendiary bombs. *SAO.*

(N.B., These figures are not on the same scale).

Introduction to the Documents

The documents in this edition are a selective sample of reports on the 'Three Nights' Blitz' on Swansea, taken from British and German sources. They are by no means a comprehensive collection: there are several other accounts, both official and unofficial, which could have been included, but were not.[1] It is felt, however, that the documents reproduced in this book give a good general impression of the events of those three nights from several points of view.

Having said that, there is not, in any case, a great deal of surviving primary source material which relates to the blitz on Swansea.[2] The great mass of wartime documentation emanating from the British central government departments was drastically weeded after the war, with the result that very little information relating to Swansea in such sources has survived in the relevant classes at the Public Record Office. The criteria for selection for retention seem to have taken into account, among other things, the importance of the target and the severity of the attack. As a relatively small provincial town, Swansea did not merit such importance as London, Birmingham, or Liverpool, while in terms of weight of attack, it sustained less punishment than these places, or towns such as Coventry or Plymouth. The records of the *Luftwaffe* similarly had a haphazard survival rate, many having been destroyed at the end of the war, those surviving having been seized by the Americans and British after the war, although some of these were later returned to the *Bundesarchiv/Militärarchiv* in Freiburg.[3] At a local level, the ARP authorities in Swansea generated extensive records in the course of their wartime activities. Some of these have survived to this day, and are held in the Swansea City Archives Office. However, great quantities of those documents were transferred from the Guildhall to outside depots in the 1950s, and were destroyed when Civil Defence was wound up in the 1960s.[4]

The documents in this edition are arranged in chronological sequence of their creation. With the exception of the newspaper reports, none of them

Figure 23. A daylight raid on Llandarcy oil refinery, probably on 10 July 1940. *SAO.*

has been previously published in its entirety. They have been faithfully transcribed as they appear in the original. Original spellings (including spelling mistakes), punctuation and capitalization have been retained, although where words are underlined in the original, they have been expressed in italics in this edition. In the list of air raids compiled by the Swansea ARP authorities, the German text of the *Luftwaffe* reports, and the reports of the Swansea AFS, lines of text have been set out exactly as in the original document. This is not the case with the other transcripts.

DOCUMENT 1.
Official List of Air Attacks on Swansea, 1940–3

This list, compiled by the ARP Department of the County Borough of Swansea, is one of several statistical lists made by that authority, which are held today in the Swansea City Archives Office. Other lists held there include detailed accounts of casualties (both killed and wounded), damaged properties, compensation for loss of or damage to property, properties requisitioned for ARP purposes, etc. Because most of these other statistical documents contain information of a personal nature, they are subject to closure until the next century.

The list of air raids is typed on three foolscap sheets of paper (33.3 cms. x 20.9 cms.), and is held in Swansea City Archives Office class P/SM 95, with another copy being classified as D.32/1. The list was started in June 1940, the last entry being made in February 1943. The heading to the first page is 'Air Raids on Swansea (1940)', that on the second and third pages is 'Air Raids on Swansea (1940–1)'. As further raids occurred, additional details were added to the list by typing. The final entry, for 16 February 1943, is entered partly in type and partly in manuscript. The casualty entries for the 'Three Nights' Blitz' omit the figures for individual nights, but give the totals for the three nights under 21 February 1941. While the total of 230 dead is correct, the total number of 397 wounded is an underestimate, the actual figure being 409.

There may have been other versions of this list bearing slightly different data, as it appears that not every known raid was entered. For instance, the 'Summary of Air Raids on the Town of Swansea' printed in K. Pryer, *Luftwaffe over Swansea* (Swansea, n.d.), pp. 10–20, which is said to be 'compiled from official sources', itemises forty-four raids, while N. Arthur, *Swansea at War* (Manchester, 1988), pp. 34–5, closely follows Pryer, but

Figure 24. German aerial photograph of a raid in progress on Llandarcy oil refinery, probably on 10 July 1940. *SAO.*

adds the raid of 20 July 1940, which is recorded in the official list and which Pryer omitted from his.

The information on each raid contained in the list is quite detailed, giving date, area attacked, casualties, quantities of bombs, and number of incidents or 'occurrences' dealt with by the ARP services. For the 'Three Nights' Blitz' the estimated total of high explosive bombs dropped during the whole three nights is given, and, at 896, is a gross underestimate, since the German sources reveal that, in fact, 1,275 high explosive bombs fell, 442 on the first night, 404 on the second night, and 429 on the third night. The figures given in press reports are also well below the actual numbers dropped, but in that case, such an underestimate may have been deliberate, with the intention of not undermining civilian morale.

The 'colours' referred to in the document relate to the system of colour-coded air raid warnings in use at the time, and the list contains only the two main stages in a system which was far more elaborate. Warnings would be picked up from a variety of sources, including the radar links and visual sightings by members of the Royal Observer Corps, and were usually transmitted by GPO telephone to the ARP Controller, who would arrange to relay them by the same means to the Divisional Controls and to local factories. Message 'yellow' meant 'preliminary caution', message 'purple' indicated that all external lights in factories had to be extinguished, and the glare from furnaces masked. Warning 'red' meant 'raiders imminent', and was the signal for sounding the sirens and taking other action. Message 'green' signified 'raiders passed', while message 'white' meant 'cancel caution' and was the signal for the 'all clear' siren to be sounded.

The list also contains a number of abbreviations, mainly relating to types of bombs. 'H.E.' stood for 'high explosive bombs' and 'I.B.' for 'incendiary bombs'. 'P.M.' indicated a 'parachute mine', while 'U.X.' or 'U.X.B.' meant 'unexploded bomb'.

DOCUMENT 2.
German Operations Reports on the 'Three Nights' Blitz'

The primary documentary sources for the study of the German *Luftwaffe* during the Second World War have been described by a leading historian as 'generally spotty',[5] since vast masses of documents were destroyed during the war or lost in the chaos which followed it. The British and Americans seized large quantities of surviving material at the end of the war for

19

Führungsabteilung
Gruppe I c

Den 21. Februar 1941.
11.35 Uhr

XR - F e r n s c h r e i b e n an:
Gr. LMS. Kurfürst, Cäsar I c,
M.Gr.Kdo. West, Lfl. 5 über Ob.d.L.

S S D - F e r n s c h r e i b e n an:
Flieger-Korps I, IV, V
Flak - Korpe II
Jafü 3, Aufkl. Gruppe 123
Lg.Kdo. VII, XII/XIII, Westfrankreich.

Zusammenstellung des Nachtangriffs vom 20./21.2.41 gegen England.

A) Einsatzstärke: 88 Flugzeuge auf S w a n s e a , davon
64 Flugzeuge über Swansea,
8 Flugzeuge über Ausweichzielen,
16 Flugzeuge abgebrochen.

B) Beobachtete Wirkung:
4 - 5 mittlere und mehrere kleinere Brände beobachtet.
Beurteilung der Wirkung:
Soweit die Wetterlage es zuliess, wurde nach Erdsicht, sonst nach Gerät abgeworfen. Es kann mit guter Trefferlage im Ziel gerechnet werden.

C) Abwehr:
Anfangs geringe Flak über Ziel, später stärker werdend.
Starke Scheinwerfertätigkeit von etwa 30 Scheinwerfern.
An engl. Südküste bei Brighton und Portsmouth schwache Flak.
Starke Flak bei Eastbourne.
Beurteilung der Abwehr:
Die Flakabwehr bei Swansea erscheint verhältnismässig gering; ebenso die Flakabwehr an der Südküste bei Brighton und Portsmouth.

D) Besondere Beobachtungen:
Etwa 10km nordwestl. Swansea ein rotes Blinklicht mit Kennung "B". In Gegend Exeter rotes Blinklicht mit Kennung "DO". 10km nördl. u. 10km ostw. des Zieles an der Küste Scheinbränd[e]
Bei Talbot (12 km südostw. Swansea) 1 beleuchtetes weisses

-9- 2

Figure 25. Page from a German Operations Report. *Bundesarchiv/Militärarchiv.*

inspection, and this also became an important basis for the publications of the official histories produced by the victorious allies since the war. Many of the captured collections have now been returned to Germany, where they reside in the *Bundesarchiv/Militärarchiv* at Freiburg, a repository which perhaps has the most complete holdings of *Luftwaffe* material.

The German operations reports on the 'Three Nights' Blitz' published in this edition are extracted from folios 14–22^{v} of file RL7/96 in the *Bundesarchiv/Militärarchiv*. They are part of the surviving records of *Luftflottenkommando 3*, the high command of the third airfleet, and form a subdivision of the records of the *Oberste Truppenkommandobehörden der Luftwaffe* (the high troop command administration of the *Luftwaffe*). They are part of an extensive series of reports on sorties by flying units against England from 1940 to 1943.

Each folio measures 20.5 cms. x 28.5 cms., and is a carbon copy of typescript on flimsy paper. Consequently, some parts of the documents are difficult to read, especially when letters such as 'a', 'e', and 'o' on the typewriter were dirty and the impression through the carbon resulted in a blob rather than a clear letter. Moreover, the reports were compiled very quickly after the bomber crews had been debriefed following their return from the sorties: there are two reports on each raid, the first one being completed between 9.30 a.m and 10.25 a.m., the second one, between 11.35 a.m. and 12.10 p.m. Consequently, there are occasional spelling mistakes, omissions of the *Umlaut*, and sometimes inconsistencies in grammar.

Both daily reports were compiled by the Operations Officer of *Luftflottenkommando 3*, a Major who signed his name as Manton or Momton. They were then sent as despatches, under the aegis of the Operations Directorate of the *Oberkommando der Luftwaffe* (*Führungsabteilung Gruppe Ic*), to a number of recipients. The recipients of the earlier report, which gave basic details of units involved and incidents which occurred, and which was described as *Kriegswichtig* ('of importance to the war'), included the group report collecting centre *'Kurfürst'*, *Cäsar Ic*, Navy Group Command West, and *Luftflotte 5*. The reports were sent as telegram despatches via the *Luftwaffe* High Command and the Paris exchange. *'Kurfürst'* was the rear echelon of the *Oberkommando der Luftwaffe*, and was located in Berlin. *'Kurfürst'* kept in close liaison with *'Robinson'*, the code-name for the forward echelon of the *Oberkommando der Luftwaffe*, which was always situated near Hitler's

Stadtplan von Swansea
mit Mil.-Geo.-Eintragungen
GB 7, BB 26
vorhandenen Unterlagen
STADTPLAN SW
NSEA (Zusammendru
SWANSEA
FOXHOLE
Zeichenerklärung
PRINCE OF WALES DOCK
RIVER TAWE
KING'S DOCK
Abkürzungen:
Grundlagen
Die Höhen sin
in engl. Fuß angegeben

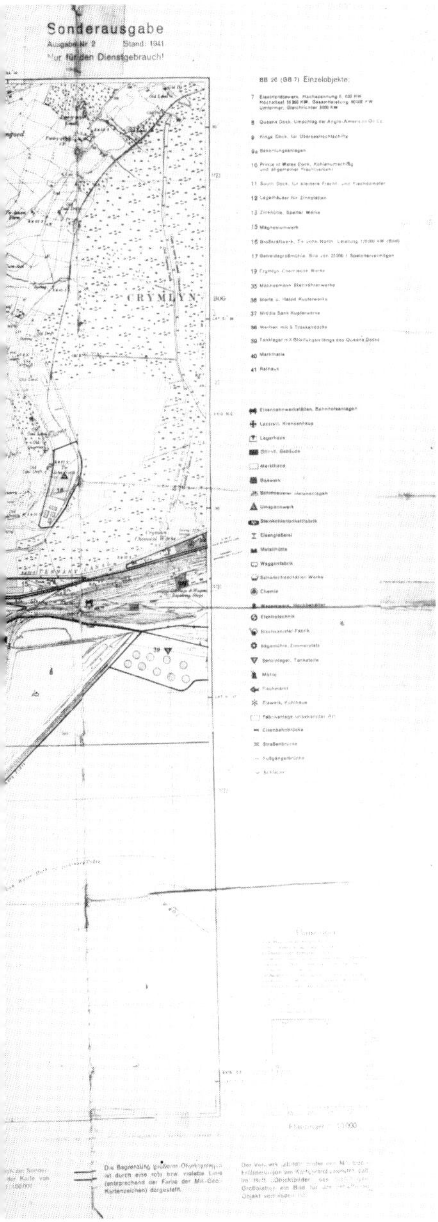

Figure 26. German target map of Swansea, 1941. *SAO.*

Replete with intelligence data of a high calibre, this map was printed at a scale of 1:10,000 and was based upon a pre-war British Ordnance Survey map. On the left-hand side of the main map, Ordnance Survey symbols are explained and translated into German. To the right of the main map are listed the principal individual targets with pictorial symbols indicating target types. Among the targets itemised are docks, factories, gasworks, railways, and the market. On the map itself, major target areas are delineated by lines (which are two-tone, in red and purple in the original). The Germans produced similar target maps for many British towns, basing them on pre-war British cartographical material which had been obtained by agents active in the United Kingdom during the 1930s.

headquarters. *'Cäsar'* was possibly the code-name of the head of the intelligence department within the *Luftwaffe* high command.[6]

The second report was a summary report, which gave totals of aircraft involved, quantities and types of bombs dropped, and contained comments on defences, the weather, losses, and any other particular observations. It was received by most of the recipients of the first report, but copies were also sent to operational units which included *Fliegerkorps I, IV*, and *V*, anti-aircraft units (*Flak Korps II*), the *Jagdfliegerführer*, or officer in charge of fighters, of *Luftflotte 3*, and *Aufklärungsgruppe 123*, a reconnaissance unit stationed near Paris. Finally, the commands of the relevant administrative air zones (*Luftgaue VII* and *XII/XIII*) in western France were also circulated.

The intelligence about raids which was despatched to these recipients was often of great practical relevance. For instance, the Do.17s and Ju. 88s of *Aufklärungsgruppe 123* were used for long range aerial photographic reconnaissance at high altitudes and had an important role to play in connexion with Swansea's 'Three Nights' Blitz'. The unit was involved in a daytime photographic reconnaissance of Swansea on 15 February 1941, and again on 24 February, flying at altitudes of 7,700 metres.[7]

Between them, the operations reports give exceptionally precise details about aircraft involved and quantities of bombs dropped on Swansea, and also about the state of defences around the town. They are not so accurate about attacks on alternative targets, since in many instances, extant British sources do not record incidents occurring at the times, dates, and places which aircrews claimed to have struck. One can therefore assume that they themselves were mistaken about precise locations, or else they jettisoned their bombs, but falsified their reports at debriefing. The reports suggest that the objective of the raids was to drop bombs in the general area of Swansea, rather than specifically to hit pre-selected sites such as the docks or industries. While the reports include mentions of strikes on specific installations such as magnesium works, gasworks, or grain mills, the repeated use of the phrase 'target area' (*Zielraum*) and occasional references to hits in the centre of 'target' (*Zielmitte*) would seem to imply that the whole of the Swansea area was the objective.

The reports also make frequent and tantalising references to dummy installations (*Scheinanlage, Scheinhafen*) and fires (*Scheinbrand*) in the vicinity of Swansea and elsewhere. These were probably decoys, such as the 'Firefly' systems which were lit when enemy aircraft approached, thereby simulating the fires caused by bombing, with the intention of luring the bombers away from their proper target. The lights flashing Morse code letters at various locations were believed by the Germans to be signals for directing British nightfighters to where the bombers were.

DOCUMENT 3.

County Borough of Swansea Auxiliary Fire Service Summary Reports

The Auxiliary Fire Service summary reports relating to incidents tackled by the Swansea AFS during the 'Three Nights' Blitz' are housed in Swansea City Archives Office, under class D.68/1. They are part of a series entitled 'Raid Summary Sheets', which give details of attacks from 1 September 1940 to 21 February 1941. The summaries are typed on sheets of paper measuring 20.5 cms. x 33 cms. The sheets for each raid were originally fastened together in the top left-hand corner by means of a pin so as to make a leaflet. The leaflets were then gathered together loose and placed inside a square-cut folder.

Figure 27. AFS personnel in the ruins of Swansea market. *SAO.*

The summary reports have been included in this edition because they provide a valuable and precise indication of where and when damage occurred on each night of the 'Three Nights' Blitz'. Such was the confusion in Swansea during these raids that most surviving statistical returns merely give totals or general details for the *whole* of the three-night period. This is the case, for example, with the summary given in the air raids list printed as Document 1. In consequence, most subsequent accounts of the 'Three Nights' Blitz' have always been somewhat vague about the timing of events.

As well as these AFS reports, there were originally other classes of document which gave similar detailed information. For instance, when incidents occurred during any raid, they were reported to the ARP Control Room by the following means. The ARP Warden on the spot would relay details to the Control Room by GPO telephone, or, if the telephone lines were damaged, messengers on bicycles or motorcycles would be used. On receipt of the message, Control Room staff would register it on an incident form, making a top copy and six carbon copies. The details in the messages would enable incidents to be plotted on a gridded plan in the Control Room, while the carbon copies were forwarded to representatives of the Auxiliary Fire Service, the Rescue and Evacuation services, the Borough Engineer, the Medical Officer of Health, and the Police Force, who would act on them as necessary. While there are a few individual message sheets still in existence, no complete known runs of these documents, or others like them, have survived to give an overall chronological picture of the events of the 'Three Nights' Blitz'.[8]

The summary reports of the AFS's activities on the first two nights give very precise indications of where and when incidents took place. However, the report for the third night notes that not all incidents were reported, for the poignant reason given. It should be noted that these summaries refer only to incidents dealt with by the Swansea AFS. The incidents tackled by 'out of town' brigades which came into Swansea to assist under the mutual aid scheme do not appear in these reports. Thus, while the picture which they give is not a totally complete one, nevertheless, the information which they do contain is of immense importance.

The Swansea Auxiliary Fire Service, founded in 1938, went out of existence in August 1941, when, it was amalgamated with the regular Swansea Police Fire Brigade, to form Area no. 21 of the National Fire Service.[9]

DOCUMENT 4.
SELECT PRESS REPORTS ON THE 'THREE NIGHTS' BLITZ'

The press reports printed here originally appeared in the *South Wales Evening Post*, the local Swansea newspaper, and are of two sorts: front page, headline reports which appeared in the newspaper on the morrow of each raid, and more 'informative' analytical reports, which appeared several days later. Neither type of report, however, contains much precise information, although the follow-up reports are more detailed, and in each of the reports Swansea is actually mentioned by name, in contrast to local press reports on earlier raids.

For the modern historian, newspapers are usually a very useful primary source, but this was not the case for wartime Swansea.[10] In common with the press all over the country, the *South Wales Evening Post* was subject to censorship under the 'D-notices' system. For nearly every raid on Swansea which it reported, the *Post* usually gave only the barest details, and seldom mentioned the town by name. Instead, euphemisms such as 'a South Wales town' or 'a Bristol Channel port' were used in reports which appeared soon after a raid had taken place, and it may have been several weeks, or even months, afterwards before a specific named reference might appear. This was because the media were allowed by the Air Ministry to name bombed towns only when it was certain that the enemy knew which place had been attacked. Even then, some newspapers, including the *South Wales Evening Post* erred on the side of caution. For example, when reporting on Swansea's final raid, the blitz of 16 February 1943, in its edition of 17 February, the *Post* described Swansea as 'a South Wales town', while on the same page, in the stop press section the newspaper cited in full a German communiqué about the raid, in which Swansea was actually named. Indeed, an identical version of the German account was published in the *Völkischer Beobachter* on 18 February 1943.[11]

As well as not naming towns, the press were prevented from naming or giving the localities of damaged buildings, although imprecise terms such as 'a school' or 'a church' might be used. A further instruction from the Press Censor meant that the fate of randomly chosen, well-known buildings might be revealed within four and eight days after a raid, if an editor chose to do so. The *South Wales Evening Post*, however, chose to exercise extreme caution and in the reports which appear here, no building is mentioned by name, although in its edition of 1 March 1941, the paper published a photograph of bomb damage, which showed St Mary's church.

Such censorship, as the Ministry of Information ceaselessly went to repeated pains to stress, was to prevent the enemy from discovering information about the results and successes of his attacks. Another, less well publicised reason, was that it was feared that reporting of precise details of raids would also have a detrimental effect on civilian morale. Paradoxically, this lack of detailed information often had the opposite result: people were confused and rumour developed, spreading easily by word of mouth, to become regarded as fact in a very short time. For instance, it was soon widely (and erroneously) believed in Swansea that the corpses of 500 persons, who had sought shelter in the Wesleyan Chapel in Goat Street, lay entombed under the rubble of that building; similarly, many believed that the emergency mortuaries had been filled to capacity, and that the Vetch Field football ground, having initially been commandeered to lay out dead bodies, was then turned into a mass grave. There is no mention of the numbers of casualties in any of the reports reproduced here, the edition of 24 February merely stating that figures were not yet available, but that casualties were not expected to be high for a raid of that size. In fact, it was not until October 1944 that the statistics relating to casualties and damage to properties were released for the first time and then they were not widely believed until reassurances about their accuracy were given in the post-war years.[12]

In comparison with press reports of earlier raids on Swansea, those following the 'Three Nights' Blitz' are unquestionably fuller, even if they still give only the barest of actual detail. The main difference between these and earlier reports is that Swansea was named from the outset. It was known that the Germans were aware that they had hit Swansea on those nights, because German press communiqués mentioned it. It was also realised that it would have been pointless to have maintained the charade of euphemisms when everyone in Swansea was more than aware that the town had been attacked, and, indeed, the glow of the fires within the blitzed area had been visible from Pembrokeshire and from north Devon, so the raids were hardly a secret. Furthermore, the scanty reporting of earlier raids had not only led to bewilderment among the population of Swansea, but had also caused a great deal of resentment. Swansea had been attacked, but was not getting public acknowledgement for its sufferings. This was a phenomenon witnessed in many other British towns, and, in response to the numerous complaints, the Ministry of Information, from time to time, published advertisements in the local and national press to inform people that their sufferings were not unrecognised, but the need to prevent the Germans from discovering such vital information was paramount.[13]

Moreover, it is probable that the lesson had been learned about the adverse effect that sparse reporting had on morale, thus a reasonably full amount of general information was given, particularly in the follow up reports on the 'Three Nights' Blitz' to prevent a further decline in morale by keeping the populace informed. Thus, many of these articles contain much more information than was previously usual, but all the facts have been carefully selected, and when read in detail, do not give very much away. If that was the intention, then it seems to have been reasonably successful, since the Mass Observation (Document 6) report implies that morale in Swansea was generally good.

One of the casualties of the 'Three Nights' Blitz' was the *South Wales Evening Post* itself. Its offices, in the former Victorian central post office situated next to the castle, were damaged by incendiaries on the third night of the blitz, and from 22 February the newspaper's editions had to be printed in Cardiff. Several of the later articles which appear here were actually dictated via the telephone to the press in Cardiff.[14]

DOCUMENT 5.

Official Report on The 'Three Nights' Blitz' by the Air Raid Precautions Controller for Swansea

This document, held in the Swansea City Archives Office, is in typescript, on eighteen sheets of paper measuring 20 cms. x 33 cms. which were originally stapled together at the top left-hand corner. The quality of the war-time paper is poor, and the document was therefore repaired by conservation staff in 1991 by re-sizing each folio and then mounting them for protection in a sewn fascicule with a protective cover, which measures 28.5 cms. x 36 cms.

The author of the report, Howell Lang Lang-Coath, had been the Town Clerk of Swansea since 1911, and continued to serve in that capacity until his retirement in 1943. He was a very competent administrator, with many years of experience of high office, and was a very forceful, sometimes autocratic, personality who ruled his staff with a rod of iron. He became ARP Controller for Swansea in April 1938, a logical step since he had been the prime mover in establishing the civil defence mechanism within the town, and the ARP Department and its ARP Officer ultimately came under the Town Clerk's control.

Figure 28.
Howell Lang Lang-Coath, ARP Controller. *SAO.*

The document is a stenographer's record of a verbal statement which Lang-Coath made to the Council of the County Borough of Swansea regarding his actions as ARP Controller during the period of the 'Three Nights' Blitz'. It seems that Lang-Coath's statement was made principally not to inform the members of the actual events of those nights, but to justify actions which he had personally taken on his own authority as Controller, without having sought approval of committee. He seems to have come under criticism from some quarters for not having called a committee to take instructions on the actions which he should have taken in response to the devastation, and there seems particularly to have been some animosity towards his arrangements for providing mobile canteens. His report is therefore peppered with strong phrases of justification for his actions, and it would appear that he was ultimately justified in these.

Lang-Coath had first reported in the same vein to the ARP Committee on 13 March, and their resolution, in minute 384, had been that he should repeat his report to full Council.[15] Following his subsequent report to their meeting on 18 March, the Council resolved to support his actions.[16] The Council were not the only ones to vindicate him. In March 1941, the government investigator, William Mabane, MP, Parliamentary Secretary to the Ministry of Home Security, who headed an enquiry into the raids and the local response to them, reported to the Home Secretary that:

> I can only attribute this [the relative success of Swansea's ARP] to the excellence of the Regional Commissioner in the preparations he has made and the manner in which the Town Clerk, Mr Lang-Coath, without any embarrassing intervention by the local Council, had taken control of the situation.[17]

Tribute was further paid to the thorough foundations laid by the County Borough of Swansea in the years leading up to the war, which enabled such an effective response from all civil defence services. Moreover, in the final analysis, the general view taken was that Lang-Coath was empowered to act in an emergency and that the massive disruption of the immediate aftermath of the raids made the calling of a committee well nigh impossible. The ultimate approval for his actions came some months later when he was awarded the CBE for the part which he had played during the emergency.

Whatever the reason for his making the statement, Lang-Coath's report provides very detailed evidence about the role of Swansea's civil defence both during the raids and in their immediate aftermath. Indeed, since it was first released in 1955, the report has been the basis of several secondary studies on the 'Three Nights' Blitz', including K. Pryer's *Luftwaffe over Swansea* and the *Western Mail's* booklet, *Bombers over Wales*, although it has never before been published in its entirety.

The report reveals the rigours and stresses of the civil defence services during the period of the emergency and shows that, despite the tribulations, that organization had a great degree of success. This may well have been attributable to the high levels of pre-war preparation, as the official line stated, but it was also in large part due to the fact that the authorities in Swansea had already had experience of two fairly severe blitzes and that organization had therefore been put to the test and had learned the lessons. The Mass-Observation report printed below comments that 'Although Swansea suffered severely from damaged utilities, organisation was more nearly adequate to cope with the various problems than in most of the blitzed towns already studied'. Another reason for the efficiency was the forcefulness of Lang-Coath's direction. Indeed, in its wider perspective, Swansea's response to the 'Three Nights' Blitz' was regarded as ranking with the best of any town in the country. For example, it stands in stark contrast to Southampton's response to its raid of 23 November 1940. There, as Tom Harrisson remarked, the

> Town Clerk stayed at his post. But he was later described as moving about in a sort of coma. Dressed in a mackintosh, he went wandering 'from group to group in gloomy activity' when he was supposed to be making decisions over a large range of blitz and post-blitz problems.[18]

Figure 29. Alderman Percy Morris, Chairman of the ARP Committee. *SAO.*

This was a far cry from the activities of Lang-Coath in Swansea, and Harrisson concluded that the main reason for the wavering in Southampton was that 'there was no outstanding personality in Southampton's government at all'.

DOCUMENT 6.
MASS-OBSERVATION REPORT ON SWANSEA

The Mass-Observation organization was established in 1937 by Tom Harrisson and Charles Madge, with the aim of carrying out research in the social sciences. In so doing, they sought to create what they termed 'an anthropology of ourselves' using two main techniques. The first was to establish a panel of volunteer 'observers' who would record their everyday lives in diaries and who replied to monthly questionnaires. The second was to set up a group of full-time investigators, based in London, but who would travel around the country observing behaviour patterns and lifestyles, etc. During the Second World War, the Ministry of Information employed this ready made chain of investigators to monitor civilian morale, particularly following air raids. The records of Mass-Observation, including the war-time ones, were placed in the library of the University of Sussex in 1970, where they today reside in the Tom Harrisson Mass-Observation Archive.[19]

The report on Swansea was compiled by a single investigator who visited the town on the Sunday following the 'Three Nights' Blitz'. He made copious notes and drawings upon which to base his report, and these are also held in the Tom Harrisson Mass-Observation Archive under reference Topic Collection, Air Raids 10/S. The report itself, comprising eleven typescript pages each measuring 20 cms. x 25.8 cms., is classified as File Reports 595.

The report provides a useful, first-hand, eye-witness account of the state of affairs in Swansea during the immediate aftermath of the 'Three Nights' Blitz', and, in many instances, it supports the evidence found in the statement of the ARP Controller. Generally, the report is complimentary about the activities of the civil defence organization in Swansea, which it states was more efficient than the organization in many other towns. The one main area of criticism, levelled both at the local ARP authorities and the Ministry of Information, was the lack of information available in the town after the attacks.

Figure 30. A policeman surveys the ruins of Castle Street. *SAO.*

Since Mass-Observation's main war-time brief was to investigate civilian morale, it is not surprising that the report concentrates very heavily on this. While it acknowledges that town 'had been shaken' by the raids and that this 'shaking' was bound to leave its permanent after effect on the population, morale was generally good, and better than in some other towns. The report ascribes this in part to the good cooperation of the authorities with the townsfolk. Interestingly, the investigator also refers to the important fact that the town centre was roped off after the raid, thus people were prevented from seeing the worst effects and damage.

The radio interview mentioned at the end of the report was broadcast on the BBC Home Service 6.00 o'clock news on 21 February 1941, and, ironically, had been intended as a tribute to the resilience of the people of Swansea. The general reaction to it in Swansea, however, had been one of hostility and indignation at what was felt to be its patronising and misleading tone. The newspaper editor, presented as a 'resident of Swansea' stated:

> there is only one subject of talk — the blitz of last night and the night before. But there are the usual smiles; even those who have lost friends and relatives are not really depressed and their stories are told in a subdued manner, but with a sense of pride .... I can honestly say that the two nights of heavy raiding here

> have not had the slightest effect on the morale of the people of Swansea ... the only effect on the spirit of the people has been to raise it higher than ever ....[20]

It was not only the people of Swansea who were upset by this, but the ARP Controller and the mayor were prompted to write formal complaints to the BBC and to the Ministry of Information, as the ARP Controller's report notes.

NOTES

1. E.g., SCA, D.32: diaries of Laurie Latchford, air raid warden in Swansea; WGRO, D/D Z 126: diary of Will Thomas, air raid warden in St Thomas, Swansea, August 1940–September 1941.
2. On sources, see J.R. Alban, *Air Raids on Swansea* (Swansea, 1981).
3. W. Murray, *Luftwaffe* (London, 1985), pp. 452–7. For holdings still in the USA, see N.A. Robins, *Eye of the Eagle. The Luftwaffe Aerial Photographs of Swansea* (Swansea, 1993).
4. Alban, *Air Raids on Swansea.*
5. Murray, *op. cit.*, p. 452.
6. A. Price, *The Luftwaffe Handbook*, pp. 9–11.
7. Robins, *op. cit.*, pp. 4–5.
8. Alban, *Air Raids on Swansea.*
9. ibid.; W.W. Hunt, *'To Guard my People'. An Account of the Origin and History of the Swansea Borough Police* (Swansea, 1957), pp. 83–91; G. Blackstone, *History of the British Fire Service* (London, 1969).
10. Alban, *Air Raids on Swansea.*
11. SAO, P/SM95.
12. *SWEP*, 24 October 1944. On war-time censorship of newspapers in general, see A. Calder, *The People's War. Britain, 1939–45* (London, 1969), esp. pp. 504–7.
13. Alban, *Air Raids on Swansea*; J. Morris, ' Morale under Air Attack: Swansea, 1939–41', *Welsh History Review*, xi, no. 3 (1983), 358–87.
14. V. Cope, 'The Short Term Effects of the "Three Nights' Blitz" on Swansea' (unpublished BEd thesis, College of St Paul and St Mary, Cheltenham, 1982), p. 39.
15. SAO, TC3/61, p. 147.
16. SAO, TC3/61, p. 138, minute 15577.
17. *SWEP*, 26 January 1972.
18. T. Harrisson, *Living through the Blitz* (London, 1976), pp. 154–5.
19. T. Jeffrey, *Mass-Observation: a Short History* (Birmingham, 1978); D. Sheridan, *The Mass-Observation Records, 1937–49* (Brighton, 1981).
20. PRO, INF 1/174.

A) *Kampfgeschwader 1.*

B) *Kampfgeschwader 26.*

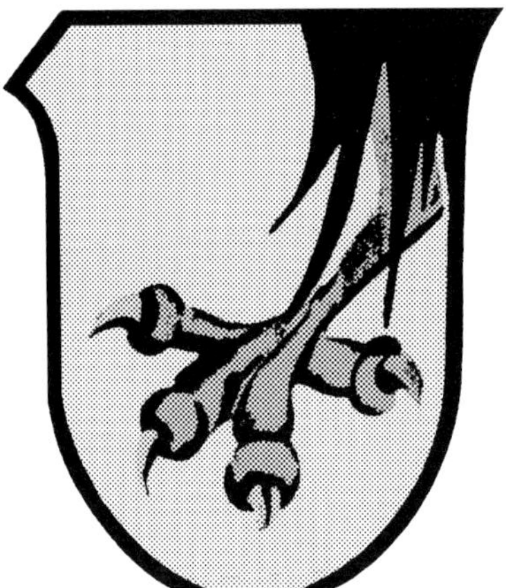

C) *Kampfgeschwader 76.*

D) *Kampfgruppe 100.*

Figure 31. Insignia of some bomber units which attacked Swansea during the 'Three Nights' Blitz'. *SAO.*

Texts of the Documents

Document 1: Official List of Air Attacks on Swansea, 1940–3, compiled by the County Borough of Swansea Air Raid Precautions Department (Swansea City Archives Office, P/SM 95 (Photographic Archive, Secondary Material: 'Blitz on Swansea') and another copy at D.32/1).

[fo. 1] ***AIR RAIDS ON SWANSEA. (1940[1]).***

DATE		COLOURS Red White	CASUALTIES Killed	Serious	Lightly	BOMBS H.E.	P.M.	No. of Occur.
1940.								
Thursday June 27.	H.E.s. & U.X.s. Danygraig Rd. & Kilvey Hill about 03.30.hrs.	No colours	–	–	–	6	–	6
Saturday June 29.	H.E.s. Llansamlet & Nr.Upper Forest Works, Morriston, early morn.	No alert	–	–	–	2	–	2
Wednesday July 10.	H.E.s. on King's Dock. 10.20. hrs.	No alert	12	13	13	4	–	1
Thursday July 18.	H.E.s. Jersey South Signal Box. Just before daylight.	00.58.02.42.	–	–	–	1	–	1
Saturday [2] July 20.	U.X. Reported Danygraig. H.E. in water alongside Fish-Market-South Dock. H.E. outside Borough Elba Cres. Early morning.	02.13.03.01.	–	–	–	2	–	2
Monday July 22.	Talefrewe Farm, Cocket. A few H.E.s. just before midnight.	22.52.02.25.	–	–	–	2	–	2
Tuesday [3] July 30.	H.E.s. Banc Mawr, Near Reddiffusion Station Cocket. early morning.	No colours	–	–	–	2	–	2
Friday August 2.	H.E.s. & I.B.s. St. James Amb. Depot. Mumbles. Foreshore Townhill, Mayhill, Treboeth. Just before and after midnight.	22.48.00.10	–	2	2	13	–	12

1. This list was begun in June 1940 and information was added to it as events took place.
2. This raid is omitted from K. Pryer's list *(Luftwaffe over Swansea. A History of the Air Attacks on Swansea, 1939–45* (Swansea, n.d.).
3. Prior: 27 July 1940: Two H.E.s dropped at the breakwater at Swansea Docks, causing slight damage. No casualties.

DATE		COLOURS Red White	CASUALTIES Killed	Serious	Lightly	BOMBS H.E.	P.M.	No. of Occur.
Saturday [1] August 10.	Fairly heavy raid Landore, Brynhyfryd, with H.E.s. in Singleton Park, Clyne & Ravenhill U.X.Bs. Just before and after midnight.	22.41.00.27.	15	5	10	30	–	21
Saturday August 3.	H.E.s. in Sea off Mumbles, I.B.s. Waunarlwydd. Just after midnight.	23.16.01.36.	–	–	–	10	–	5
Saturday [2] August 17.	H.E:s. & U.X.s. in moderate Raid in Cwmbwrla, Greenhill, Treboeth & parts of Strand. Early morning.	01.36.02.17.	–	4	8	30	–	11
Sunday August 18.	H.E.s. & U.X.B.s. in moderate raids in Gors Avenue, Greenhill, Cwmbwrla and Foxhole. Early morning.	No alert	1	2	1	12	–	7
Saturday August 24.	I.B.s. on Kilvey Hill, Pt. Tennant, St. Thomas & Killay. No serious fires. Alert & Raiders past was given, together with bombs falling between the two warnings dusk raid.	20.45.21.37. 21.38.22.50.	–	–	–	–	–	7
Sunday Sept. 1 & 2.	BLITZ	29.51.03.16.	33	37	71	106	–	219

1. Prior: 6 August 1940: Ten H.E.s in the sea at West Cross. No casualties.
2. Prior: 16 August 1940: Twenty H.E.s in the sea off Mumbles Head.

[fo. 2] ***AIR RAIDS ON SWANSEA. (1940 – 41.)***

DATE		COLOURS Red White	CASUALTIES Killed	Serious	Lightly	BOMBS H.E.	P.M.	No. of occur.
1940								
Thursday [1] Sept. 5.	U.X.B. Tyrhester Farm, Llansamlet & Treboeth. Just before midnight.	22.08.02.28.	–	–	–	4	–	2
Wednesday Sept. 11.	H.E. & U.X.B. Langland Ter. & Cheshyre St. Brynmill. Just before 9.pm.	21.11.00.08.	–	–	–	2	–	2
Tuesday Sept. 24.	I.B.s. & Petrol Bomb in Centre of Town & South Dock Area. No serious fires. Just before 11.PM.	21.02.23.41.	–	–	–	–	–	29
Wednesday Sept. 25.	H.E.s. & U.X.B.s. & I.Bs. High St. Area. Mt. Pleasant Mayhill, Townhill, Uplands, St. Thomas also report of Petrol Bomb. Just after dusk.	20.50.21.42.	–	–	–	9	–	21
Wednesday Oct. 9.	H.E.s. & I.B.s. Kilvey Hill & North District. Just after dusk.	18.58.20.52.	–	–	–	6	–	12
Monday Oct. 21.	H.E.s. & U.X.B.s. Gors Avenue. Mayhill. Llansamlet. Also small number I.B.s. at Llansamlet. Just before midnight.	19.26.00.20.	–	–	–	15	–	11
1941								
Thursday Jan. 2.	Two small H.E.s. in field at Ynystawe. Just before midnight.	18.53.23.58.	–	–	–	2	–	2
Sunday [2] Jan. 5.	H.E.s. & U.X.B.s. Dillwyn St. St. Helens Rd. Sketty Park Est. St. Thomas, and a few I.B.s. in town & St. Thomas. Just after midnight.	23.41.06.46.	–	7	13	12	–	22

1. Prior: 3 August 1940: Two H.E.s dropped in Crumlin Brook. 4 August 1940: Four H.E.s dropped on farmland at Llansamlet. Three exploded, one went off the following day. No damage or casualties.
2. Prior wrongly gives this date as 4 January.

DATE		COLOURS Red White	CASUALTIES Killed	Serious	Lightly	BOMBS H.E.	P.M.	No. of Occur.
Monday Jan. 13.	A lone plane with lights on dropped bombs in King's Dock. Just after 10.PM.	No colours	–	–	5	2	–	2
Friday Jan. 17.	BLITZ	19.10.04.06.	55	38	59	178	–	170
Wednesday Feb. 19.	BLITZ	19.37.23.59.	( )	( )	( )	( )	–	187
Thursday Feb. 20.	BLITZ	19.48.00.24.	( )	( )	( )	( )	–	172
Friday Feb. 21.	BLITZ	19.30.00.40.	230.	260.	137.	896	–	228
Monday [1] March 3.	H.E.s. Banc Mawr Cockett Open fields. Just before 11.pm.	No colours	–	–	–	6	–	6

1. Prior describes a raid on this date as 'one slight casualty occurred when four H.E.s. were dropped at Cefn Coed'. He also refers to a raid on 4 March 1940: Twelve H.E.s dropped on the foreshore between Mumbles and Swansea. No damage or casualties.

o. 3]

AIR RAIDS ON SWANSEA. (1940 – 41).

DATE		COLOURS Red White	CASUALTIES Killed	Serious	Lightly	BOMBS. H.E.	P.M.	No. of Occur.
1941 Wednesday March 12.	Stick of H.E.s. in Neath Rd. Near Bridge Inn about 9.30.pm.	21.52.02.23.	3	2	4	16	–	4
Friday March 14.	Large number of I.B.s. in Bonymaen. No fires. About midnight.	20.20.03.16.	–	–	–	–	–	2
Monday March 24.	Early evening Raid – Daylight H.E.s. Danygraig Road.	17.29.18.41.	–	–	–	4	–	3
Monday March 31.	H.E.s. on Strand Power House. Very rough night. Just after 9.PM.	20.58.21.20.	3	–	–	2	–	1
Tuesday April 8.	I.B.s. & H.E.s. Mumbles Head & Limeslade. Gorse Fires. Early morning.	21.07.04.13.	–	–	–	1	–	4
Tuesday April 22.	Parachute Mines – 1.U.X. – Frederick Place. Llansamlet. About Midnight.	23.19.00.21.	–	–	13	–	2	2
Tuesday [1] May 20.	H.E.s. Neath Rd. School. Morriston. One just outside Borough. A little after midnight.	23.24.02.00.	–	–	3	1	–	1
Saturday May 31.	H.E.s. Pengwine Rd. Treboeth Morriston. Just after midnight.	00.36.04.13.	–	–	4	4	–	3
Saturday June 28.	H.E.s. Cliff Walk – Langland Bay & U.X.B. Mayhill Gdns. Early morning.	01.44.03.11.	–	–	–	4	–	2
Friday Nov. 28.	Two parachute mines – Strand & Burrows – Pt. Tennant. About 9.PM.	19.06.21.03.	1	7	13	–	2	2
1943 [2] Tuesday Feb. 16.	BLITZ	22.04 23.00	34	61	50			

1. Prior gives this date as 29 May 1941.
2. Prior: 2 July 1942: approximately 240 incendiaries fell in the Birchgrove area. No damage or casualties.

Document 2: German Operations Reports on the 'Three Nights' Blitz' on Swansea (*Bundesarchiv/ Militärarchiv*, Freiburg, class RL7/96 (*Oberste Truppenkommandobehörden der Luftwaffe: Lagemeldungen über den Luftangriff auf Swansea*, fos. 14–22^{v})).

[fo. 14] Führungsabteilung
Gruppe Ic

Den 20. Februar 1941
10.05 Uhr

KR — Fernschreiben an:

Gr. LMS Kurfürst, Cäsar Ic, M.Gr. Kdo. West,
Lfl. 5 über Ob.d.L. und W = Leit 3 über L.V. Paris

Einzelmeldung Nr. 1 vom 20.2.1941.

A) Luftlage:
Zu 2 a): *Erfolgsmeldung zum Nachteinsatz vom 19./20.2.1941*

Angriff auf Swansea.

Angegriffen haben und waren über Ziel:

IV. Flieger Korps:

I. /K.G.27 — durch 8 He 111 zwischen 21.29 – 21.35 Uhr aus 2700 – 3500 m Höhe mit 4 SC 500, 23 SC 250, 94 SC 50. Mehrere kleinere Brände beobachtet, weitere Beobachtung durch Wolken behindert.

II./K.G.27 — durch 10 He 111 zwischen 21.25 – 22.15 Uhr aus 2500 – 4000 m Höhe mit 10 SC 250, 20 SC 250 LZZ, 80 SC 50. Bomben in Zielraum, Wirkung nicht beobachtet.

III./K.G.27 — durch 7 He 111 zwischen 20.39 – 21.50 Uhr aus 2600 – 3600 m Höhe mit 16 SC 250, 60 SC 50. Abwurf teilweise mit Erdsicht. Masse der Bomben in Zielraum, 3 größere und 2 kleinere Brandherde beobachtet.

Document 2: German Operations Reports on the 'Three Nights' Blitz' on Swansea (*Bundesarchiv/ Militärarchiv*, Freiburg, class RL7/96 (*Oberste Truppenkommandobehörden der Luftwaffe: Lagemeldungen über den Luftangriff auf Swansea*, fos. 14–22[v])).

o. 14] Operations Section — 20 February 1941
[Central Command Luftwaffe] Group I c [1] — 10.05 hrs.

KR — Despatches to:

Group Report Collecting Centre, Kurfürst, Cäsar Ic, Navy Group Command West, Air Fleet 5 via Luftwaffe High Command and Distribution 3 via Paris exchange

---

Report no. 1 of 20.2.1941.

A) Air Situation:

to 2a): *Success Report on the Night Operation of 19./20.2. 1941.*

Attack on Swansea.

[Units which] attacked and were over target:

IV. Flieger Korps [2]:

I./Kampfgeschwader 27 — by 8 He. 111s between 21.29 – 21.35 hrs. [3] from 2,700 – 3,500 metres altitude with 4 SC 500s, 23 SC 250s, 94 SC 50s. Several small fires observed, further observation hindered by clouds.

II./Kampfgeschwader 27 — by 10 He. 111s between 21.25 – 22.15 hrs. from 2,500 – 4,000 metres altitude, with 10 SC 250s, 20 SC 250 LZZs, 80 SC 50s. Bombs in target area. Effect not observed.

III./Kampfgeschwader 27 — by 7 He. 111s between 20.39 – 21.50 hrs. from 2,600 – 3,600 metres altitude with 16 SC 250s, 60 SC 50s. Release partly by sight of ground. Bulk of the bombs in the target area, 3 larger and 2 smaller fire locations observed.

1. Translator's note: in the two *Meldungen* of 20 February 1941 the recipients and sender are translated in full, but thereafter are referred to only by their German initials or titles.
2. Since there were no British equivalents to the *Luftwaffe* units referred to in this text, they have remained untranslated. On this first page of the translation the unit abbreviations have been extended. On subsequent pages they appear in their original abbreviated form.
3. The times cited in these German documents were one hour ahead of contemporary British time.

K.Gr.100 — durch 8 He 111 zwischen 21.02 – 21.22 Uhr mit 7680 B1 El, 1536 B1 El ZA. Abwurf erfolgte einwandfrei nach Gerät, Lage alle Bomben dicht zusammen, 1 großer, 2 mittler und mehrere kleine Brände beobachtet.

K.Gr.606 — durch 10 Do 17 zwischen 21.45 – 22.40 Uhr aus 2700 – 3300 m Höhe mit 100 SC 50, 600 B1 El. Aufschläge größtenteils beobachtet, davon 5 mit Brandwirkung.

[fo. 14v] *I. Flieger Korps:*

K.G.1 — durch 11 He 111 und 7 Ju 88 zwischen 22.25 – 00.03 Uhr aus 1700 – 3800 m Höhe mit 4 SC 1000, 6 SC 500, 31 SC 250, 14 SC 250 LZZ, 5904 B1 El. Abwurf erfolgte größtenteils mit Erdsicht. Trefferlage gut in Zielraum, 3 große und mehrere kleinere Brände beobachtet.

Ferner wurden angegriffen:

IV. Flieger Korps:
Plymouth:

III./K.G.27 — durch 1 He 111 (wegen Ausfall der Umpumpanlagen) um 20.20 Uhr aus 3800 m Höhe mit 20 SC 50. Einschläge im Ostteil der Stadt. Wirkung nicht beobachtet.

K.Gr.100 — durch 1 He 111 (Ausfall des Sondergeräts) um 20.45 Uhr mit 960 B1 El, 192 B1 El ZA. Wirkung nicht beobachtet.

50 km nordostwärts Plymouth:

III./K.G.27 — durch 1 He 111 (Motor-Ölverlust, Nachlassen der Motore) um 21.35 Uhr aus 3500 m Höhe mit 4 SC 250. Wirkung nicht beobachtet.

Kampfgruppe 100	by 8 He. 111s between 21.02 – 21.22 hrs. with 7,680 B1 Els, 1,536 B1 El ZAs. Release achieved without problem by apparatus. [1] Position of all bombs close together, 1 larger, 2 medium, and several small fires observed.
Kampfgruppe 606	by 10 Do. 17s between 21.45 – 22.40 hrs. from 2,700 – 3,300 metres altitude with 100 SC 50s, 600 B1 Els. Impacts for the most part observed, of which 5 developed into fires.

). 14v] *I. Flieger Korps:*

K.G. 1	by 11 He.111s and 7 Ju. 88s between 22.25 – 00. 03 hrs. from 1,700 – 3,800 metres altitude with 4 SC 1000s, 6 SC 500s, 31 SC 250s, 14 SC 250 LZZs, 5,904 B1 Els. Release achieved for the most part through ground sighting. Strikes good in target area, 3 large and several smaller fires observed.

Further were attacked:

IV. Flieger Korps:
Plymouth [2]*:*

III./K.G. 27	by 1 He. 111 (due to failure of circulation pump) at 20.20 hrs. from 3,800 metres altitude with 20 SC 50s. Hits in the east part of the town. Effect not observed.
K.Gr. 100	by 1 He. 111 (failure of special equipment) at 20.45 hrs. with 960 B1 Els, 192 B1 El ZAs. Effect not observed.

50 kilometres north-eastwards of Plymouth:

III./K.G. 27	by 1 He. 111 (engine oil loss, power loss in engine) at 21.35 hrs. from 3,500 metres altitude with 4 SC 250s. Effect not observed.

1. This refers to the *X-Gerät* bombing system installed in the aircraft of K.Gr. 100. III./K.G. 26 used the alternative *Y-Verfahren* system.
2. This attack is confirmed in the official list of raids on Plymouth. See H.P. Twyford, *It Came to Our Door* (Plymouth, 1946), who relates that on the night of 19 February 1941, 'between 7.15 and 10.30, when a strong force of German bombers, numbering between fifty and seventy-five, were on their way to South Wales, about a dozen high explosive bombs were dropped in the area of Valletort Road, Stoke, and Stonehouse town hall. There was some damage to property, and one person subsequently died from injuries, while three others had to receive treatment'.

Southampton:
I. Flieger Korps:
K.G.1 durch 2 Ju 88 (wegen Motorstörung und Störung an Umpump-Anlage) um 22.50 Uhr aus 3800 m Höhe mit 1 SC 1000, 3 SC 500, 1 SC 250 LZZ. Abwurf erfolgte nach Sicht. Wirkung nicht beobachtet.

Brighton:
K.G.1 durch 1 Ju 88 (wegen Motorstörung) um 21.30 Uhr aus 4000 m Höhe mit 1 SC 1000, 1 SC 250. Wirkung nicht beobachet.

Umgebung von Portland:

IV. Flieger Korps:
I./K.G.27 durch 1 He 111 (Notwurf wegen Ausfall der Umpump-Anlage) um 20.50 Uhr aus
[fo. 15] 5000 m Höhe mit 1 SC 500, 1 SC 250, 8 SC 50. Wirkung nicht beobachtet.

Abgebrochen haben:

1 He 111 der II./K.G.27 (wegen Blockieren der Bedienungshebel durch Vereisen)
1 He 111 der III./K.G.27 (wegen Motorschaden)
1 Do 17 der K.Gr.606 (wegen Ölverlust).

Zu 2 b): Geringe Flakabwehr an Südküste bei Plymouth und am Ziel. Starke Flakabwehr bei Southampton. An Südküste und bei Swansea geringe bis starke Scheinwerfertätigkeit. Über Ziel 1 Nachtjäger, über Bristol-Kanal 2 Nachtjäger ohne Angriff. Über Swansea Sperrballone in 1600 – 2000 m Höhe.

Zu 1 b): Eigene Verluste keine.

Sonstiges: Am Ziel erwartates Wetter 5/10 Bewölkung, tatsächlich war 9/10 und 10/10, zeitweise 6/10 Bewölkung.

Lfl. Kdo.3, Gruppe Ic:
I.A.
Manton
Major

Southampton [1]*:*
I. Flieger Korps:
K.G. 1 — by 2 Ju. 88s (due to engine malfunction and malfunction of circulation pump) at 22.50 hrs. from 3,800 metres altitude with 1 SC 1000, 3 SC 500s, 1 SC 250 LZZ. Successful release by sight. Effect not observed.

Brighton [2]*:*
K.G. 1 — by 1 Ju.88 (due to engine malfunction) at 21.30 hrs. from 4,000 metres altitude with 1 SC 1000, 1 SC 250. Effect not observed.

Vicinity of Portland:
IV. Flieger Korps:
I./K.G. 27 — by 1 He. 111 (emergency jettisoning due to failure of circulation pump) at 20.50 hrs. from
. 15] 5,000 metres altitude with 1 SC 500, 1 SC 250, 8 SC 50s. Effect not observed.

Broken off:
1 He. 111 of the II./K.G. 27 (due to blocking up of the operating lever, through icing up)
1 He. 111 of the III./K.G. 27 (due to engine damage)
1 Do. 17 of K.Gr. 606 (due to oil loss).

To 2 b): Limited flak defences on South Coast around Plymouth and at the target. Strong flak defence near Southampton. On South Coast and around Swansea light to heavy searchlight activity. Over target 1 nightfighter, over Bristol Channel 2 nightfighters without attack. Over Swansea barrage balloons at 1,600 – 2,000 metres altitude.

To 1 b): Own losses nil.

Special remarks: At the target expected weather 5/10 clouding, actually was 9/10 and 10/10, for a time 6/10 clouding.

Airfleet Command 3, Group I c
Operations Officer
Manton
Major

1. The official file giving accounts of all air raids on Southampton, with statistics, does not record a raid for this date (Southampton Record Office, SC/CD2/1).

2. There is no record of a raid on Brighton on this date. Indeed, many of the claimed attacks on alternative targets mentioned below cannot be substantiated from British records. However, where incidents below are noteworthy of further comment, a footnote has been added.

[fo. 15v] BLANK

[fo. 16] Führungsabteilung
Gruppe Ic

Den 20. Februar 1941.
11.35 Uhr

KR — Fernschreiben an:

Gr. LMS Kurfürst, Cäsar Ic,
M.Gr. Kdo. West, Lfl. 5 über der Ob.d.L.

SSD — Fernschreiben an:

Flieger Korps I, IV, V
Flak-Korps II
Jafü 3, Aufkl.Gruppe 123
Lg.Kdo. VII, XII/XIII, West-Frankreich.

Zusammenstellung des Nachtangriffs vom 19./20.2.1941 gegen England.

A) *Einsatzstärke:* *71 Flugzeuge auf Swansea,* davon

61 Flugzeuge über Swansea,
7 Flugzeuge über Ausweichzielen,
3 Flugzeuge abgebrochen.

B) *Beobachtete Wirkung:*

3 größere, 2 mittlere und mehrere kleinere Brände beobachtet.

Beurteilung der Wirkung:

Am Ziel erwartates Wetter 5/10 Bewölkung, tatsächlich angetroffe 9/10 – 10/10, zeitweise 6/10 Bewölkung.
Abwurf: Soweit es die Wetterlage zuliess, teilweise mit Erdsicht. Wenn auch eine größere Wirkung nicht ausgemacht werden konnte, kann donnoch mit einer teilweisen guten Trefferlage gerechnet werden.

C) *Abwehr:*

Geringe Flakabwehr an Südküste bei Plymouth und am Ziel. Starke Flakabwehr bei Southampton. An Südküste und bei Swansea geringe bis starke Scheinwerfertätigkeit. 1 Nachtjäger über Ziel, über Bristol-Kanal 2 Nachtjäger ohne Angriff. Über Swansea Sperrballone in 1600 – 2000 m Höhe.

Beurteilung der Abwehr:

Die Abwehr kann im allgemeinen als ziemlich schwach angesehen werden.

. 15v] BLANK

o. 16] Operations Section 20 February 1941.
[Central Command Luftwaffe] Group I c 11.35 hrs.

KR — Despatches to:

Group Report Collecting Centre Kurfürst, Cäsar I c,
Navy Group Command West, Airfleet 5 via Luftwaffe
High Command.

SSD — Despatches to:

Flieger-Korps I, IV, V
Anti-Aircraft Corps II
Fighter Leader Airfleet 3, Reconnaissance Group 123
Air Zone Command VII, XII/XIII, Western France.

Summary Report of the Night Attack of 19./20.2.1941 against England.

A) *Operational Strength: 71 aircraft for Swansea,* of which:

61 aircraft over Swansea,
7 aircraft over alternative targets,
3 aircraft aborted.

B) *Observed Effects:*

3 larger, 2 medium and several smaller fires observed.

Evaluation of the effects:
At the target expected weather 5/10 clouding, actually found to be 9/10 – 10/10, for a time 6/10 clouding.
Release: so far as the weather conditions permitted it, partially by sight of ground. If a greater effect is not certain, one can reckon on at least a partially good hit.

C) *Defences:*

Light flak defences at South Coast near Plymouth and at the target. Strong flak defences near Southampton. On South Coast and near Swansea light to heavy searchlight activity. 1 nightfighter over target, over Bristol Channel 2 nightfighters without attack. Over Swansea barrage balloons at 1,600 – 2,000 metres altitude.

Evaluation of the defences:
The defences can, in general, be regarded as pretty feeble.

D) *Besondere Beobachtungen:*

Westlich Bristol im Bristol-Kanal 1 Scheinanlage.

6 – 8 km südöstlich Swansea bei Port-Talbot 1 großer Scheinbrand.

[fo. 16v] Über Swansea wurden von 3 Besatzungen rötliche, sich horizontal schnell bewegende Leuchtkörper in 2000 m Höhe beobachtet.

Bei Port Hawl [*sic*] vermutlich 1 Scheinhafen mit roter Hindernis-Beleuchtung und weissem Landekreuz.

1 gleiche Anlage bei Shepron-Mallet [*sic*].

E) *Abgeworfene Bombenmenge:*

Auf Swansea:	49,2 to Sprengbomben	u. 15,72 to B1 El
Auf Ausweichziele:	7,15 to " "	u. 1,152 to B1 El

Zusammenstellung der auf England abgeworfenen Bombenmenge:

	Davon auf Swansea:
6 SC 1000	4 SC 1000
14 SC 500	10 SC 500
91 SC 250	80 SC 250
15 SC 250 LZZ	14 SC 250 LZZ
362 SC 50	334 SC 50
15144 B1 El	14184 B1 E1
1728 B1 El ZA	1536 B1 El ZA

F) *Eigene Verluste:*

Keine.

Lfl.Kdo. 3, Gruppe Ic:
I.A.

Manton

Major

D) *Particular Observations:*

West of Bristol in the Bristol Channel 1 dummy works.

6 – 8 kilometres south-east of Swansea near Port Talbot 1 larger decoy fire.

. 16^{v}] Over Swansea a reddish, fast moving horizontal body of light at 2,000 metres altitude was observed by 3 crews.

Near Port Hawl [*sic*] supposedly 1 dummy airfield with red obstacle light and white landing cross.

1 similar lay-out near Shepron-Mallet [*sic*].

E) *Bomb Loads Dropped:*

On Swansea: 49.2 tonnes of high explosive bombs and 15.72 tonnes of B1 Els. [1]

On alternative targets: 7.15 tonnes of high explosive bombs and 1.152 tonnes of B1 Els.

Summary of Bomb Loads dropped on England:

	of which on Swansea:
6 SC 1000s	4 SC 1000s
14 SC 500s	10 SC 500s
91 SC 250s	80 SC 250s
15 SC 250 LZZs	14 SC 250 LZZs
362 SC 50s	334 SC 50s
15,144 B1 Els	14,184 B1 Els
1,728 B1 El ZAs	1,536 B1 El ZAs

F) *Own Losses:*

None.

Airfleet Command 3, Group I c:
Operations Officer

Manton

Major

1. i.e., incendiary bombs. See chapter on German bombs, pp. 41–4.

[fo. 17] Führungsabteilung Den 21. Febr. 1941.
Gruppe Ic 10.25 Uhr

KR — Fernschreiben an:

Gr. LMS. Kurfürst, Cäsar Ic, M.Gr. Kdo. West,
Lfl.5 über Ob. d. L. und W-Leit 3 über L.V. Paris.

Einzelmeldung Nr. 1 vom 21.2.1941.

A) Luftlage:
Zu 2a): Erfolgsmeldung zum Nachteinsatz vom 20./21.2.1941.

Angriff auf Swansea.

Angegriffen haben und waren über Ziel:
IV. Flieger-Korps:

I. K.G. 27 durch 7 He 111 zwischen 21.15 und 21.40 Uhr aus 3200 – 4000 m Höhe mit 5 SC 500, 14 SC 250 und 52 SC 50. Mehrere kleine Brände und Explosionen beobachtet.

II. K.G.27 durch 8 He 111 zwischen 21.00 und 21.40 Uhr aus 2800 – 3500 m Höhe mit 8 SC 250, 16 SC 250 LZZ und 64 SC 50. Abwurf nach Sicht. Mehrere Brände, 1 Explosion mit Rauchwolken beobachtet.

III.K.G. 27 durch 7 He 111 zwischen 21.07 und 21.14 Uhr aus 2500 – 3700 m Höhe mit 12 SC 250, 3 SC 250 LZZ und 67 SC 50. Abwurf nach Sicht; Brandherd beobachtet.

K.Gr.100 durch 11 He 111 zwischen 21.02 und 21.36 Uhr aus 6800 m Höhe mit 10560 B1 El. und 2112 B1 El.ZA. Abwurf nach Gerät. 1 grosser, 2 mittlere und mehrere kleine Brände beobachtet.

o. 17] Führungsabteilung
Gruppe I c

21 February 1941.
10.25 hrs.

KR -—Despatches to:

Gr. LMS. Kurfürst, Cäsar Ic, M. Gr. Kdo. West,
Lfl. 5 via Ob. d. L. and W-Leit 3 via L.V. Paris.

Report no. 1 of 21.2.1941.

A) Air Situation:
To 2 a): *Success Report on the Night Operation of 20./21.2.1941.*

Attack on Swansea.

[Units which] attacked and were over target:
IV. Flieger-Korps:

I. K.G. 27 — by 7 He. 111s between 21.15 and 21.40 hrs. from 3,200 – 4,000 metres altitude with 5 SC 500s, 14 SC 250s and 52 SC 50s. Several small fires and explosions observed.

II. K.G. 27 — by 8 He. 111s between 21.00 and 21.40 hrs. from 2,800 – 3,500 metres altitude with 8 SC 250s, 16 SC 250 LZZs and 64 SC 50s. Release by sight. Several fires, 1 explosion with smoke cloud observed.

III. K.G. 27 — by 7 He. 111s between 21.07 and 21.14 hrs. from 2,500 – 3,700 metres altitude with 12 SC 250s, 3 SC 250 LZZs and 67 SC 50s. Release by sight; seat of fire observed.

K. Gr. 100 — by 11 He. 111s between 21.02 and 21.36 hrs. from 6,800 metres altitude with 10,560 B1 Els and 2,112 B1 El ZAs. Release by apparatus. 1 larger, 2 medium and several small fires observed.

I. Flieger-Korps:

K.G. 1 durch 7 He 111 und 4 Ju 88 zwischen 22.50 und 23.50 Uhr aus 2500 – 3800 m Höhe mit 2 SC 1000, 11 SC 500, 23 SC 250, 11 SC 250 LZZ und 4032 B1 El. Abwurf nach Sicht. Mehrere Explosionen im Ziel Swansea, Getreidegrossmühle, beobachtet. In Gegend Gaswerk heftige Explosionen mit weissem Feuerschein und starker [fo. 17v] Rauchentwicklung. Treffer in Bahn- und Hafenanlage nördl. Magnesiumwerk Swansea und in Stadtmitte. 5 grosse und 8 kleine Brände mit Sicherheit erkannt.

II.K.G.76 durch 7 Ju 88 zwischen 22.28 und 22.45 Uhr aus 1800 – 3200 m Höhe mit 14 SC 250 und 70 SD 50.

I. u. III. K.G.77 durch 8 Ju 88 zwischen 23.07 und 00.45 Uhr aus 3800 – 4000 m Höhe mit 5 SC 500, 22 SC 250 und 10 AB 36. Brände beobachtet.

III.K.G.26 durch 5 He 111 zwischen 22.24 und 23.08 Uhr aus 4000 m Höhe mit 5 SC 500, 2880 B1 El. Abwurf nach Y-Verfahren. Ziel von 3 Besatzungen erkannt. Es wurden erst 5 dann 8 Brände festgestellt.

Ferner wurden angegriffen:

IV. Flieger-Korps:

K.G.27 *Portland:* durch 1 He 111 (wegen Ausfall Peilgeräts) um 20.45 Uhr aus 3400 m Höhe mit 4 SC 250 und 16 SC 50. Wirkung nicht beobachtet.

I. Flieger-Korps:

K.G.1 *Portsmouth:* durch 1 He 111 (wegen FT-Ausfall) um 23.30 Uhr aus 4000 m Höhe mit 3 SC 250, 1 SC 250 LZZ und 584 B1 El. Brände beobachtet.

Eastbourne: durch 1 Ju 88 (wegen Hydraulik-Schaden) um 21.35 Uhr aus 3800 m Höhe mit 3 SC 500. Brandherd beobachtet.

Brighton: durch 1 Ju 88 (wegen Ausfall der Umpumpanlage) um 21.40 Uhr aus 3500 m Höhe mit 1 SC 1000 und 1 SC 250 LZZ. Starke Explosion und Brandentwicklung beobachtet.

I. Flieger-Korps:

K.G. 1 — by 7 He. 111s and 4 Ju. 88s between 22.50 and 23.50 hrs. from 2,500 – 3,800 metres altitude with 2 SC 1000s, 11 SC 500s, 23 SC 250s, 11 SC 250 LZZs and 4,032 B1 Els. Release by sight. Several explosions on the Swansea target, grainmill observed. In vicinity of the gasworks violent explosions with white fire glare [. 17v] and stronger smoke development. Hits in railway and dock areas to the north of Swansea Magnesium works and in town centre. 5 large and 8 small fires known for certain.

II. K.G. 76 — by 7 Ju. 88s between 22.28 and 22.45 hrs. from 1,800 – 3,200 metres altitude with 14 SC 250s and 70 SD 50s.

I. and III. K.G. 77 — by 8 Ju. 88s between 23.07 and 0.45 hrs. from 3,800 – 4,000 metres altitude with 5 SC 500s, 22 SC 250s and 10 AB 36s. Fires observed.

III. K.G. 26 — by 5 He. 111s between 22.24 and 23.08 hrs. from 4,000 metres altitude with 5 SC 500s and 2,880 B1 Els. Release by *Y-Verfahren*. Target recognised by 3 crews. They confirmed first 5 then 8 fires.

Further were attacked:

IV. Flieger-Korps:

K.G. 27 — *Portland:* by 1 He. 111 (due to failure of direction finding equipment) at 20.45 hrs. from 3,400 metres altitude with 4 SC 250s and 16 SC 50s. Effect not observed.

I. Flieger-Korps:

K.G. 1 — *Portsmouth:* by 1 He. 111 (due to radio failure) at 23.30 hrs. from 4,000 metres altitude with 3 SC 250s, 1 SC 250 LZZ and 584 B1 Els. Fires observed.

Eastbourne: by 1 Ju. 88 (due to hydraulics damage) at 21.35 hrs. from 3,800 metres altitude with 3 SC 500s. Seat of fire observed.

Brighton: by 1 Ju. 88 (due to failure of circulation pump) at 21.40 hrs. from 3,500 metres altitude with 1 SC 1000 and 1 SC 250 LZZ. Strong explosion and development of fire observed.

II. K.G.76 *Cardiff:* durch 1 Ju 88 (wegen Verlust der Bl [illegible] kappe) um 21.35 Uhr aus 3100 m Höhe. Angriff auf Hafenanlage Cardiff mit 2 SC 250 und 10 SD 50. Keine Wirkungsbeobachtung.

Bridgewater: durch 1 Ju 88 (wegen fehlender Erdsicht über eigentlichem Ziel) um 21.45 Uhr aus 1900 m Höhe mit 2 SC 250 u. 10 SD 50. Keine Wirkungsbeobachtung.

[fo. 18] K.G.77 *Bristol:* durch 1 Ju 88 (wegen Motorschaden) um 22.45 Uhr aus 4000 m Höhe mit 1 SC 500 u. 3 SC 250. Keine Wirkungsbeobachtung.

Southampton: durch 1 Ju 88 (wegen Schaden an der Umpumpanlage) um 00.05 Uhr aus 4000 m Höhe mit 1 SC 500 und 3 SC 250. Kleinere Brände in Hafenviertel beobachet.

Abgebrochen haben:

1 He 111 der I.K.G.27 (wegen Schaden des linken Motors)
1 He 111 der II.K.G.27 (wegen Ausfall d. FT-Anlage)
2 He 111 " III.K.G.27 (wegen starker Vereisung)
2 He 111 " K.Gr.100 (wegen Vereisung)

2 He 111 u.
1 Ju 88 des K.G.1 (wegen FT-Ausfall und Schaden an Umpumpanlage)
6 Ju 88 des K.G.77 (2 wegen Vereisung, 1 wegen Ölverlust, 1 wegen Peiler-Ausfall, 1 wegen Motorschaden u. 1 wegen Fahrwerkschaden).
1 He 111 der III.K.G.26 (wegen Ausfall des FT-Geräts).

II. K.G.76 — *Cardiff:* by 1 Ju. 88 (due to loss of the [illegible]) at 21.35 hrs. from 3,100 metres altitude. Attack on dock installation at Cardiff with 2 SC 250s and 10 SD 50s.[1] No effects observed.

Bridgwater[2] : by 1 Ju. 88 (due to loss of sight of ground over the proper target) at 21.45 hrs. from 1,900 metres altitude with 2 SC 250s and 10 SD 50s. No effects observed.

fo. 18] K.G. 77 — *Bristol:* by 1 Ju. 88 (due to engine damage) at 22.45 hrs. from 4,000 metres altitude with 1 SC 500 and 3 SC 250s. No effects observed.

Southampton: by 1 Ju. 88 (due to damage to the circulation pump) at 00.05 hrs. from 4,000 metres altitude with 1 SC 500 and 3 SC 250s. Smaller fires in the harbour quarter observed.

Broken off:

1 He. 111 of the I. K.G. 27 (due to damage to the port engine)
1 He. 111 of the II. K.G. 27 (due to radio failure)
2 He. 111s of the III. K.G. 27 (due to heavy icing)
2 He. 111s of the K.Gr. 100 (due to icing)

2 He. 111s and
1 Ju. 88 of the K.G. 1 (due to radio failure and damage to circulation pump)
6 Ju. 88s of the K.G. 77 (2 due to icing, 1 due to oil loss, 1 due to failure of direction finding equipment, 1 due to engine damage and 1 due to landing-gear damage).
1 He. 111 of the III. K.G. 26 (due to radio failure).

1. Despite the precise detail of this claim, there is no record of such an attack on that date.

2. The A.R.P. records for Bridgwater for the whole period of the 'Three Nights' Blitz' make no reference to local incidents there. Indeed, under 19, 20, and 21 February 1941 the sole entry in the A.R.P. Diary of Incidents for Somerset notes 'Raid on Swansea' (Somerset Record Office, C/CD/Gen Box 3/27). The Register of Messages, December 1940 – April 1941 (ibid., box 6/64), however, records the following information for 20 February 1941:

Time	*District*	*Message*
17.04	Bridgwater	Situations report nil
20.37	Taunton	Report of flares or IB near Chard
21.16	Bathavon	UXB report
21.56	Taunton	Re explosion
23.10	Taunton	Report of bright orange light

Zu 2 b): Geringe schwere Flak bei Swansea, im allgemeinen gut liegend, später etwas starker werdend. Bei Swansea etwa 30 Scheinwerfer mit starker Tätigheit. An engl. Südküste schwache Flakabwehr. Bei Brighton geringe Flak. Swache Flak und einige Scheinwerfer bei Portsmouth; starke Flak bei Eastbourne.

Zu 3 b): *Verluste:* keine.

Lfl.Kdo.3, Gruppe Ic:

Manton

Major

[fo. 18[v]] BLANK

To 2 b): Trifling heavy flak near Swansea, in general lying well, later becoming somewhat stronger. At Swansea about 30 searchlights with strong activity. On English South Coast weak flak defences. Near Brighton trifling flak. Feeble flak and some searchlights by Portsmouth; strong flak by Eastbourne.

To 3 b): *Losses:* None.

Lfl. Kdo. 3 Gruppe I c:

Manton

Major

o. 18v] BLANK

[fo. 19] Führungsabteilung
Gruppe Ic

Den 21. Februar 1941.
11.35 Uhr

KR — Fernschreiben an:
Gr. LMS. Kurfürst, Cäsar Ic,
M.Gr.Kdo. West, Lfl. 5 über Ob.d.L.

SSD — Fernschreiben an:
Flieger-Korps I, IV, V
Flak-Korps II
Jafü 3, Aufkl. Gruppe 123
Lg.Kdo. VII, XII/XIII, Westfrankreich.

Zusammenstellung des Nachtangriffs vom 20./21.2.41 gegen England.

A) *Einsatzstärke:*

88 Flugzeuge auf Swansea, davon
64 Flugzeuge über Swansea,
8 Flugzeuge über Ausweichzielen,
16 Flugzeuge abgebrochen.

B) *Beobachtete Wirkung:*

4 – 5 mittlere und mehrere kleinere Brände beobachtet.
Beurteilung der Wirkung:

Soweit die Wetterlage es zuliess, wurde nach Erdsicht, sonst nach Gerät abgeworfen. Es kann mit guter Trefferlage im Ziel gerechnet werden.

C) *Abwehr:*

Anfangs geringe Flak über Ziel, später stärker werdend. Starke Scheinwerfertätigkeit von etwa 30 Scheinwerfern. An engl. Südküste bei Brighton und Portsmouth schwache Flak. Starke Flak bei Eastbourne.
Beurteilung der Abwehr:
Die Flakabwehr bei Swansea erscheint verhältnismässig gering; ebenso die Flakabwehr an der Südküste bei Brighton und Portsmouth.

[fo. 19] Führungsabteilung
Gruppe I c

21 February 1941.
11.35 hrs.

KR — Despatches to:
Gr. LMS Kurfürst, Cäsar I c,
M. Gr. Kdo. West, Lfl. 5 via Ob. d. L.

SSD — Despatches to:
Flieger-Korps I, IV, V
Flak-Korps II
Jafü 3, Aufkl. Gruppe 123
Lg. Kdo. VII, XII/XIII, Western France.

Summary Report of the Night Attack of 20./21.2.41 against England.

A) *Operational Strength:*

88 aircraft for Swansea, of which
64 aircraft over Swansea,
8 aircraft over alternative targets,
16 aircraft broke off.

B) *Observed Effects:*

4 – 5 medium and several smaller fires observed.
Evaluation of the effects:
As far as the weather conditions permitted it, [bombs] were released by ground sight, or else by apparatus. Good hits on the target can be reckoned.

C) *Defences:*

Beginning light flak over target, later becoming heavier. Strong searchlight activity from about 30 searchlights. On English South Coast near Brighton and Portsmouth weak flak. Heavy flak by Eastbourne.
Evaluation of the defences:
The flak defences near Swansea appeared relatively limited; the same as the flak defences on the South Coast by Brighton and Portsmouth.

D) *Besondere Beobachtungen:*

Etwa 10 km nordwestl. Swansea ein rotes Blinklicht mit Kennung "B". In Gegend Exeter rotes Blinklicht mit Kennung "DO". 10 km nördl. u. 10 km ostw. des Zieles an der Küste Scheinbrände. Bei Talbot (12 km südostw. Swansea) 1 beleuchtetes weisses
[fo. 19^{v}] "T" (6 Lampen in ostwärtiger Richtung, 2 Querlampen im Westen).

D) *Abgeworfene Bombenmenge:*

Auf Swansea:	58,40 to. Sprengbomben,	17,832 B1 El.
		u. 2,112 B1 El ZA.
Auf Ausweichziele:	10,05 to. "	u. 0,584 B1 El.

Zusammenstellung der auf England abgeworfenen Bombenmenge:

	davon auf Swansea:
3 SC 1000	2 SC 1000
31 SC 500	26 SC 500
110 SC 250	93 SC 250
32 SC 250 LZZ	30 SC 250 LZZ
199 SC 50	183 SC 50
90 SD 50	70 SD 50
18416 B1 El.	17832 B1 El.
2112 B1 El. ZA.	2112 B1 El. ZA.

E) *Eigene Verluste:*

1 He 111 der III.K.G.27	vor Landung abgestürzt (Aufschlagbrand - 3 Mann tot, 1 schwer verletzt)
1 He 111 der I.K.G.27	im unbesetzten franz. Gebiet abgestürzt (Besatzung abgesprungen).

Lfl.Kdo. 3, Gruppe Ic:

Manton

Major

D) *Particular Observations:*

About 10 kilometres north-west of Swansea a red flashing light with Morse code character 'B'. In the Exeter area red flashing light with Morse code character 'DO'. 10 kilometres north and 10 kilometres east of the target on the coast decoy fires. By [Port] Talbot (12 kilometres south-east of Swansea) 1 [fo. 19^{v}] illuminated white "T" (6 lamps in an eastwards direction, 2 transverse lamps in the westwards).

D) *Bomb loads dropped:*

On Swansea: 58.40 tonnes of high explosive bombs, 17,832 B1 Els. and 2,112 B1 El ZAs.

On alternative targets: 10.05 tonnes of high explosive bombs and 0,584 B1 Els.

Summary of bomb loads dropped on England:

	of which on Swansea:
3 SC 1000s	2 SC 1000s
31 SC 500s	26 SC 500s
110 SC 250s	93 SC 250s
32 SC 250 LZZs	30 SC 250 LZZs
199 SC 50s	183 SC 50s
90 SD 50s	70 SD 50s
18,416 B1 Els	17,832 B1 Els
2,112 B1 El ZAs	2,112 B1 El ZAs.

E) *Own losses:*

1 He. 111 of the III. K.G. 27	crashed before landing (fire on impact — 3 men dead, 1 badly wounded)
1 He. 111 of the I. K.G. 27	crashed in the French unoccupied zone (crew baled out).

Lfl.Kdo. 3 Gruppe I c:

Manton

Major

[fo. 20] Führungsabteilung
Gruppe Ic

Den 22. Februar 1941.
9.30

KR — Fernschreiben an:
Gr. LMS Kurfürst, Casär Ic, M-Gr. Kdo. West, Lfl. 5
über Ob.d.L. und W-Leit 3 über L.V. Paris.

Einzelmeldung Nr. 2 vom 22.2.1941.

A) Luftlage:
Zu 2 a): *Erfolgsmeldung zum Nachteinsatz vom 21./22.2.1941*

Angriff auf Swansea:

Angegriffen haben und waren über Ziel:
IV. Flieger Korps:

I./K.G.27	durch 8 He 111 zwischen 20.50 – 22.30 Uhr. Ziel aus 3000 – 4800 m Höhe mit 3 SC 500, 21 SC 250, 94 SC 50, 4 LC 50 angegriffen. Bomben lagen im befohlenen Zielraum. 2 größere Explosionen, sonst keine besondere Wirkung erkannt.
II./K.G.27	durch 7 He 111 zwischen 21.12 – 22.15 Uhr aus 2600 – 3500 m Höhe mit 19 SC 250, 2 SC 250 LZZ, 48 SC 50, 16 LC 50. Bomben lagen in Zielraum. Explosionen und 1 große Brand in Stadtmitte beobachtet.
III./K.G.27	durch 8 He 111 zwischen 21.10 – 22.05 Uhr aus 2000 – 2400 m Höhe mit 8 SC 250, 120 SC 50, 4 LC 50. Abwurf größtenteils nach Erdsicht, 1 große Explosion in Stadtmitte, etwa 10 kleinere Brände über Stadtgebiet verteilt beobachtet.
K.Gr.100	durch 12 He 111 zwischen 21.28 – 22.02 Uhr aus 6800 m Höhe mit 11059 B1 El, 2765 B1 El ZA. Abwurf nach Gerät. Lage der Brandfelder in Zielmitte. 8 große Brände und 15 mittlere Brände beobachtet.
K.Gr.606	durch 7 Do 17 zwischen 22.11 – 23.35 Uhr aus 2800 – 3500 m Höhe mit 70 SC 50, 420 B1 El. Abwurf nach Erdsicht, Aufschläge im Zielraum und westlich Stadtmitte beobachtet, davon 4 mit Brandwirkung

[No. 20] Führungsabteilung
Gruppe I c

22 February 1941.
9.30

KR — Despatches to:
Gr. LMS Kurfürst, Cäsar Ic, M-Gr. Kdo. West, Lfl. 5
via Ob. d. L. and W-Leit via L.V. Paris.

Report no. 2 of 22.2.1941.

A) Air Situation:
To 2 a): Success Report on the Night Operation of 21./22.2.1941

Attack on Swansea:

[Units which] attacked and were over target:
IV. Flieger Korps:

I./K.G. 27	by 8 He. 111s between 20.50 – 22.30 hrs. Target attacked from 3,000 – 4,800 metres altitude with 3 SC 500s, 21 SC 250s, 94 SC 50s, 4 LC 50s. Bombs positioned in the ordered target area. 2 larger explosions, otherwise no particular effect observed.
II./K.G. 27	by 7 He. 111s between 21.12 – 22.15 hrs. from 2,600 – 3,500 metres altitude with 19 SC 250s, 2 SC 250 LZZs, 48 SC 50s, 16 LC 50s. Bombs positioned in target area. Explosions and 1 large fire observed in town centre.
III./K.G. 27	by 8 He. 111s between 21.10 – 22.05 hrs. from 2,000 – 2,400 metres altitude with 8 SC 250s, 120 SC 50s, 4 LC 50s. Release mostly by sight of ground, 1 large explosion in town centre, about 10 smaller fires distributed over town area observed.
K. Gr. 100	by 12 He. 111s between 21.28 – 22.02 hrs. from 6,800 metres altitude with 11,059 B1 Els, 2,765 B1 El ZAs. Release by apparatus. The fire fields lay in the target centre. 8 large fires and 15 medium fires observed.
K. Gr. 606	by 7 Do. 17s between 22.11 – 22.35 hrs. from 2,800 – 3,500 metres altitude with 70 SC 50s, 420 B1 Els. Release by sight of ground, impacts observed in the target area and western town centre, of which 4 observed resulted in fire

[fo. 20v] und großen Explosionen, im Ziel und Stadt zahlreiche Brandbombenherde und 10 – 12 größere Brände beobachtet.

Flieger Korps I:

K.G.1 durch 6 He 111 und 5 Ju 88 zwischen 22.55 – 01.00 Uhr aus 2200 – 3400 m Höhe mit 10 SC 500, 31 SC 250, 7 SC 250 LZZ, 3600 B1 El. Abwurf nach Erdsicht bei geringer Bewölkung. Großer Brand in Stadtmitte, 7 Flächenbrände im Westteil und über 20 kleinere Brändstellen erkannt.

III./K.G.26 durch 6 He 111 zwischen 22.47 – 23.49 Uhr aus 3800 – 4000 m Höhe mit 6 SC 500, 2592 B1 El. Abwurf bei rasch wechselnder Bedeckung, nicht immer nach Sicht möglich. 1 Besatzung zählte über 30 Brände. 4 Großbrände westlich des Y-Strahles.

Ferner wurden angegriffen:

IV. Flieger Korps:

I./K.G.27 *Bournemouth:* durch 1 He 111 (wegen Motorstörung) um 20.50 Uhr aus 4000 m Höhe mit 1 SC 500, 2 SC 250 und 8 SC 50. Wirkung wegen Dunst nicht erkannt.

III./K.G.27 *Plymouth:* durch 1 He 111 (wegen starken Schütteln 1 Motors) um 20.40 Uhr aus 2200 m Höhe mit 4 SC 250. Abwurf nach Erdsicht. 2 Bomben hart ostw. Eisenbahnbrücke über Cattewater. 1 Brand hervorgerufen. 2 Bomben im Nordwestteil der Stadt. Ein größerer roter Brand.

Abgegbrochen haben:

1 He 111 der II./K.G.27	(Ausfall 1 Motors, Flugzeug 3 km SW Caen abgestürzt.)
1 He 111 " II./K.G.27	(Starkes Nachlassen beider Motore, Besatzung bei Valognes abgesprungen.)
1 He 111 " III./K.G.27	(Ausfall des linken Motors)
1 He 111 " K.G.[*sic*]100	(Wegen Vereisung)

). 20[v]]

and large explosions, in the target and town numerous incendiary bomb fires and 10 – 12 larger fires observed.

Flieger Korps I:

K.G. 1 by 6 He. 111s and 5 Ju. 88s between 22.55 – 01.00 hrs. from 2,200 – 3,400 metres altitude with 10 SC 500s, 31 SC 250s, 7 SC 250 LZZs, 3,600 B1 Els. Release by sight of ground through thin cloud. Larger fire in town centre, 7 sheet fires in the western part and over 20 smaller fires perceived.

III./K.G. 26 by 6 He. 111s between 22.47 – 23.49 hrs. from 3,800 – 4,000 metres altitude with 6 SC 500s, 2,592 B1 Els. Release through rapidly changing cloud cover not always possible by sight. 1 crew counted over 30 fires. 4 large fires west of the Y-beam.

Further were attacked:

IV. Flieger Korps:

I./K.G. 27 *Bournemouth:* by 1 He. 111 (due to engine damage) at 20.50 hrs. from 4,000 metres altitude with 1 SC 500, 2 SC 250s and 8 SC 50s. Effect not observed owing to haze.

III./K.G. 27 *Plymouth:*[1] by 1 He. 111 (due to strong vibration of 1 engine) at 20.40 hrs. from 2,200 metres altitude with 4 SC 250s. Release by sight of ground. 2 bombs close to east of the railway line above Cattewater. 1 fire broke out. 2 bombs in the north-west part of the town. 1 larger red fire.

Broken off:

1 He. 111 of the II./K.G. 27 (failure of engine, aircraft crashed 3 kilometres south-west of Caen.)
1 He. 111 of the II./K.G. 27 (strong decline in both engines. Crew baled out near Valognes.)
1 He. 111 of the III./K.G. 27 (failure of the port engine)
1 He. 111 of the K.G. [*sic*] 100 (due to icing)

1. Despite the detail of this claim, there is no record of such an attack on this date among British sources.

[fo. 21] 2 He 111 und 1 Ju 88 des K.G.1

1 He 111 Ausfall des Bordnetzes.
1 He 111 Kühlerschaden.
Ju 88 Ausfall der Blindfluginstrumente.

Zu 2 b) Abwehr:

In niedrigen Höhen starke, überfallartige Flak, in größeren Höhen geringe Flak.
Rege Scheinwerfertätigkeit von etwa 30 Scheinwerfern.
Mehrere Sperrballone in 1800 m Höhe.
Um 22.10 Uhr 2 Nachtjäger ohne Angriff. 1 Nachtjäger über Kanal etwa 40 km südl. Start Point. Ein einmot. Jäger um 20.30 Uhr Angriffversuch, jedoch kein Beschuß.

Lfl. Kdo. 3 Gruppe Ic
I.A.

Manton

Major

[fo. 21v] BLANK

o. 21] 2 He. 111s and 1 Ju. 88 of the K.G. 1

1 He. 111 failure of on-board electrical circuits.
1 He. 111 radiator damage.
Ju. 88 failure of blind flying instruments.

To 2 b) Defences:

In lower altitudes strong, surprise flak, in greater altitudes weak flak.
Brisk activity by about 30 searchlights.
Several barrage balloons at 1,800 metres altitude.
At 22.10 hrs. 2 nightfighters without attack. 1 nightfighter over Channel about 40 kilometres south of Start Point. One single-engined fighter attempted to attack at 20.30 hrs., however, did not open fire.

Lfl. Kdo. 3 Gruppe I c:
Operations Officer

Manton

Major

. 21[v]] BLANK

[fo.22] Führungsabteilung
Gruppe Ic

Den 22. Februar 1941
12.10

KR – Fernschreiben an:
Gr. LMS Kurfürst, Cäsar I c
M.Gr.Kdo. West, Lfl.5 über Ob.d.L.

SSS [sic] – Fernschreiben an:
Flieger Korps I, IV, V
Flak Korps II
Jafü 3, Aufkl. Gruppe 123
Lg. Kdo. VII, XII/XIII, Westfr.

Zusammenstellung des Nachtangriffs vom 21./22.2.41 gegen England.

A) *Einsatzstärke:*

68 Flugzeuge auf Swansea, davon
59 Flugzeuge über Swansea
2 Flugzeuge über Ausweichziele
7 Flugzeuge abgebrochen.

B) *Beobachtete Wirkung:*

In Stadtmitte 1 große Explosion mit anschließendem großem Brand, sowie 7 Flächenbrände im Westteil der Stadt und weitere etwa 20 kleinere Brände im gesamten Stadtgebiet beobachtet.

Beurteilung der Wirkung:
Da größtenteils mit Erdsicht abgeworfen wurde, kann mit guter Trefferlage im Ziel gerechnet werden.

C) *Abwehr:*

In niedrigen Höhen starke, überfallartige Flak, in größeren Höhen geringe Flak.
Rege Scheinwerfertätigkeit von etwa 30 Scheinwerfern.
Mehrere Sperrballone in 1800 m Höhe.
Um 22.10 Uhr 2 Nachtjäger ohne Angriff. 1 Nachtjäger über Kanal etwa 40 km südl. Start Point. Ein einmot. Jäger um 20.30 Uhr Angriffversuch, jedoch kein Beschuß.

fo.22] Führungsabteilung
Gruppe I c

22 February 1941
12.10

KR – Despatches to:
Gr. LMS Kurfürst, Cäsar I c
M. Gr. Kdo. West, Lfl. 5 via Ob. d. L.

SSS [sic] – Despatches to:
Flieger Korps I, IV, V
Flak Korps II
Jafü 3, Aufkl. Gruppe 123
Lg. Kdo. VII, XII/XIII, Western France.

Summary Report of the Night Attack of 21./22.2.41 against England.

A) *Operational Strength:* *68 aircraft for Swansea*, of which
59 aircraft over Swansea
2 aircraft over alternative targets
7 aircraft broken off.

B) *Observed Effects:*

In town centre 1 large explosion with resulting large fire, as well as 7 sheet fires in the west part of the town and, further, about 20 smaller fires in the whole town district observed.

Evaluation of the effects:
Since for the most part release was by sight of ground, good hits on the target can be reckoned.

C) *Defences:*

In low altitudes heavy, surprise flak, at greater altitudes weak flak.
Busy searchlight activity from about 30 searchlights.
Several barrage balloons at 1,800 metres altitude.
At 22.10 hrs. 2 nightfighters without attack. 1 nightfighter over Channel about 40 kilometres south of Start Point. One single-engined fighter at 20.30 hrs. attempting attack, however did not open fire.

[fo. 22v] *Beurteilung der Abwehr:*
Die Flakabwehr bei Swansea ist gegenüber den Vortagen scheinbar etwas stärker geworden, doch immer noch verhältnismäßig gering.

D) *Besondere Beobachtungen:*

Scheinbrände: 10 km SW Swansea.
Südl. Swansea ein brennendes Schiff.
50 km südl. Swansea.

Leuchtfeuer: 15 km nördl. Exeter rot "S"
Westl. Exeter rot "U"
Ostw. davon 1 weisses Leuchtdreieck und ein Platz mit Nachtflugbetrieb.
5 km südl. Ilfracombe rot "O D"
St. Athan rot "O T" mit weissem Dauerlicht.
Nördl. Swansea rot "P E"
südl. Cardiff rot "S"

E) *Abgeworfene Bombenmenge:*

Auf Swansea 47,6 Sprengbomben und 17,671 to B1 El
2,765 to B1 El ZA.

Bournemouth	1,4	"
Plymouth	1,0	"
	50,0	"

Zusammenstellung der auf England abgeworfenen Bombenmenge:

	Davon auf Swansea:
20 SC 500	19 SC 500
85 SC 250	79 SC 250
9 LZZ250	9 LZZ250
330 SC 50	322 SC 50
17671 B1 El	17671 B1 El
2765 B1 El ZA	2765 B1 El ZA.

F) *Eigene Verluste:*

1 He 111 der II./K.G.27 auf Rückflug bei Aunay-sur-Odon (30 km südwestl. Caen) abgestürzt. Besatzung 1 Mann tot, 4 Mann verletzt.

1 He 111 der II./K.G.27 auf Rückflug in gegend Valognes (bei Cherbourg) abgestürzt. Besatzung 1 Mann leichtverletzt, 4 Mann unverletzt.

Lfl. Kdo.3 Gruppe I c:
I.A.
Manton
Major

[Fo. 22v] *Evaluation of the defences:*
The flak defence at Swansea, in contrast to previous days, has apparently become stronger, yet it is still relatively weak.

D) *Particular observations:*

Decoy fires:	10 kilometres south-west of Swansea. South of Swansea a burning ship. 50 kilometres south of Swansea.
Beacons:	15 kilometres north of Exeter red 'S' west of Exeter red 'U' Eastwards of which 1 white light triangle and a place with night flying activity. 5 kilometres south of Ilfracombe red 'O D' St Athan red 'O T' with white permanent light. North of Swansea red 'P E' South of Cardiff red 'S'

E) *Bomb loads dropped:*

On Swansea	47.6 [tonnes of] high explosive bombs and 17,671 tonnes *[sic]* B1 Els. 2,765 tonnes *[sic]* B1 El ZAs.
Bournemouth	1.4 [tonnes of] high explosive bombs
Plymouth	1.0 [tonnes of] high explosive bombs
	50.0 [tonnes of] high explosive bombs

Summary of bomb loads dropped on England:

	of which on Swansea:
20 SC 500s	19 SC 500s
85 SC 250s	79 SC 250s
9 LZZ 250s	9 LZZ 250s
330 SC 50s	322 SC 50s
17,671 B1 Els	17,671 B1 Els
2,765 B1 El ZAs	2,765 B1 El ZAs.

E) *Own losses:*
1 He 111 of the II./K.G. 27 crashed on the return flight near Aunay-sur-Odon (30 kilometres south-west of Caen). Crew: 1 man dead, 4 men injured.
1 He. 111 of the II./K.G. 27 crashed on the return flight in the vicinity of Valognes (near Cherbourg). Crew: 1 man slightly injured, 4 men uninjured.

Lfl. Kdo. 3 Gruppe I c:
Operations Officer

Manton

Major

Document 3: County Borough of Swansea Auxiliary Fire Service Summary Reports relating to the 'Three Nights' Blitz' on Swansea (Swansea City Archives Office, D.68/1 (Swansea A.F.S. Records)).

[fo. 1] *COUNTY BOROUGH OF SWANSEA.*

AUXILIARY FIRE SERVICE.

SUMMARY OF FIRES ATTENDED – ENEMY ACTION 19.2.41/20.2.41.

Premises.	*Description of Premises.*	*Damage Incurred.*
INCIDENT NO. 1. TIME 2005.		
91, Rhondda Street.	Dwelling House.	First Landing. (Slight).
CAUSE OF FIRE – INCENDIARY BOMB. PUMP/S IN ATTENDANCE: 1 L.T.[1] (33).		
FIRE EXTINGUISHED BY SAND.		
INCIDENT NO. 2. TIME 2005.		
Tawe Lodge, Mount Pleasant.	Infirmary.	Nil.
CAUSE OF FIRE – INCENDIARY BOMB. PUMP/S IN ATTENDANCE: 1 L.T. (34).		
INCIDENT NO. 3. TIME 2006.		
Eddershaws & Aplins, Northampton Lane.	Furniture Depository and General Stores.	Slight.
CAUSE OF FIRE – INCENDIARY BOMB. PUMP/S IN ATTENDANCE: 1 L.T. (41).		
INCIDENT NO. 4. TIME 2008.		
Oliver Watkin's Yard, Rockland Terrace.	Timber Yard.	Building Partly Destroyed.
CAUSE OF FIRE – INCENDIARY BOMB. PUMP/S IN ATTENDANCE: 1 L.T. (42).		
INCIDENT NO. 5. TIME 2010.		
Blind Institution, Northampton Place.	Institution.	Minor.
CAUSE OF FIRE – INCENDIARY BOMBS. PUMP/S IN ATTENDANCE: 1 L.T. (49).		
INCIDENT NO. 6. TIME 2010.		
23, Manor Road, Manselton.	Dwelling House.	Damage to front bedroom & clothing, etc.
CAUSE OF FIRE – INCENDIARY BOMB. PUMP/S IN ATTENDANCE: 1 L.T. (6).		

1. Light trailer pump.

[fo. 2] *Continuation No. 1.*

Premises.	*Description of Premises.*	*Damage Incurred.*
INCIDENT NO. 7. TIME 2010.		
70, Manor Road, Manselton.	Garage.	Slight Damage to Garage. Fire Damage to car.
CAUSE OF FIRE – INCENDIARY BOMBS.	*PUMP/S IN ATTENDANCE: 1 L.T. (43).*	
INCIDENT NO. 8. TIME 2012.		
Masonic Hall, St. Helen's Road.	Hall.	Nil.
CAUSE OF FIRE – INCENDIARY BOMBS.	*PUMP/S IN ATTENDANCE: 1 L.T. (40).*	
INCIDENT NO. 9. TIME 2014.		
Stores Timber Yard, South Dock.	Stores.	Nil.
CAUSE OF FIRE – INCENDIARY BOMBS.	*PUMP/S IN ATTENDANCE: 1 L.T. (23).*	
INCIDENT NO. 10. TIME 2015.		
61, Norfolk Street, Mount Pleasant.	Dwelling House.	Bedroom Wall badly burnt & partly demolished.
CAUSE OF FIRE – INCENDIARY BOMBS. *FIRE EXTINGUISHED BY STIRRUP PUMP.*	*PUMP/S IN ATTENDANCE: 1 L.T. (4).*	
INCIDENT NO. 11. TIME 2015.		
43, Rhondda Street, Mount Pleasant.	Dwelling House.	Hole in roof, floorboard of bedroom damaged.
CAUSE OF FIRE – INCENDIARY BOMBS.	*PUMP/S IN ATTENDANCE: 1 L.T. (4).*	
INCIDENT NO. 12. TIME 2017.		
Pell Street.	Dwelling House.	No Fire.
CAUSE OF FIRE –	*PUMP/S IN ATTENDANCE:.1 L.T. (26).*	
INCIDENT NO. 12. [sic]. TIME 2018.		
St. Helen's Road, William Street.	Y.M.C.A.	No trace of fire. No trace of fire.
CAUSE OF FIRE –	*PUMP/S IN ATTENDANCE: 1 L.T. (30).*	
INCIDENT NO. 13. TIME 2018.		
70, William Street.	Dwelling House.	House partly burnt.
CAUSE OF FIRE – INCENDIARY BOMBS.	*PUMP/S IN ATTENDANCE: 1 L.T. (24).*	

[fo. 3] *Continuation No. 2.*

Premises.	*Description of Premises.*	*Damage Incurred.*
INCIDENT NO. 14. TIME 2019.		
"Hazelmere", Pentregethin Road, Caerethin.	Dwelling House.	Few tiles and part of guttering.
CAUSE OF FIRE – INCENDIARY BOMBS.	*PUMP/S IN ATTENDANCE: 1 L.T. (20).*	
INCIDENT NO. 15. TIME 2020.		
Cambrian Institute, Mount Pleasant.	Private Institution.	Minor.
CAUSE OF FIRE – INCENDIARY BOMBS.	*PUMP/S IN ATTENDANCE: 1 L.T. (39).*	
INCIDENT NO. 16. TIME 2020.		
2, Eaton Crescent. Also several houses in Eaton Crescent.	Dwelling House.	Minor in each case.
CAUSE OF FIRE – INCENDIARY BOMBS.	*PUMP/S IN ATTENDANCE: 1 L.T. (48).*	
INCIDENT NO. 17. TIME 2024.		
Henrietta Street, (George Hotel and Jordan's Garage, Duke Street).	Hotel and Motor Garage.	Extensive.
CAUSE OF FIRE – INCENDIARY BOMBS.	*PUMP/S IN ATTENDANCE: 1 L.T. (37). 1 H.T.[1] (9).*	
INCIDENT NO. 18. TIME 2025.		
20 & 22, Caebricks Road.	Dwelling House.	Two Houses damaged, but some of the furniture saved.
CAUSE OF FIRE – INCENDIARY BOMBS.	*PUMP/S IN ATTENDANCE: 1 L.T. (43).*	
INCIDENT NO. 19. TIME 2025.		
(77 Eaton Road,	Dwelling House.	)
(2 Cross Street,	" "	)
(Brynhyfryd Street,	" "	Extensive.)
(Llangyfelach Road,	" "	)
(Treboeth Hall.	Public Hall.	)
CAUSE OF FIRE – INCENDIARY BOMBS.	*PUMP/S IN ATTENDANCE: 1 L.T. (45).*	
INCIDENT NO. 20. TIME 2026.		
Day's Garage, St. Helen's Road.	Garage.	Nil.
CAUSE OF FIRE – INCENDIARY BOMBS.	*PUMP/S IN ATTENDANCE: 1 H.T. (2).*	
NO ACTION TAKEN BY SKETTY CREW.		

1. Heavy trailer pump.

[fo. 4] *Continuation No. 3.*

Premises.	*Description of Premises.*	*Damage Incurred.*
INCIDENT NO. 21. TIME 2028.		
Cwmfelyn Schools, Cwmbwrla.	Schools.	Nil.
CAUSE OF FIRE –		*PUMP/S IN ATTENDANCE: 1 L.T. (14).*
INCIDENT NO. 22. TIME 2030.		
Manselton Auxiliary Fire Station.	Fire Station.	Hole in Roof, bedding and Office Wall.
CAUSE OF FIRE – INCENDIARY BOMBS.		*PUMP USED – STIRRUP PUMP AND APPLICATION SAND.*
INCIDENT NO. 23. TIME 2030.		
Oliver Watkin's, Walter Road.	Furniture Store and Offices.	Minor.
CAUSE OF FIRE – INCENDIARY BOMBS.		*PUMP/S IN ATTENDANCE: STIRRUP PUMP.*
INCIDENT NO. 24. TIME 2030.		
53, Oxford Street.	Dwelling House.	Slight Damage to Bedroom.
CAUSE OF FIRE – INCENDIARY BOMBS. FIRE EXTINGUISHED BY STIRRUP PUMP.		*PUMP/S IN ATTENDANCE: 1 L.T. (23).*
INCIDENT NO. 25. TIME 2031.		
(74, Geriol Road, (Mayhill.	Dwelling House.	Wardrobe & Chairs burnt.
(75, Geriol Road, (Mayhill.	Dwelling House.	Bed, Ceiling, Roof and small amount of furniture burnt.
CAUSE OF FIRE – INCENDIARY BOMBS.		*PUMP/S IN ATTENDANCE: 1 L.T. (34).*
INCIDENT NO. 26. TIME 2033.		
Eden Avenue, Uplands.	Dwelling House.	Nil.
CAUSE OF FIRE – INCENDIARY BOMB. FIRE OUT ON ARRIVAL OF CREW.		*PUMP/S IN ATTENDANCE: 1 L.T. (50).*
INCIDENT NO. 27. TIME 2037.		
Duke Street, Swansea.	Garage.	Building gutted.
CAUSE OF FIRE – INCENDIARY BOMBS.		*PUMP/S IN ATTENDANCE: 1 L.T. (49).*
INCIDENT NO. 28. TIME 2037.		
Approach Road, Manselton.		No Fire.
CAUSE OF FIRE –		*PUMP/S IN ATTENDANCE: 1 L.T. (17).*

[fo. 5] *Continuation No. 4.*

Premises.	*Description of Premises.*	*Damage Incurred.*

INCIDENT NO. 29. TIME 2040.

Pentrechwyth Road, Near Gwindy Inn.	Dwelling House.	Nil.

CAUSE OF FIRE – INCENDIARY BOMB. PUMP/S IN ATTENDANCE: 1 L.T. (29). NO ACTION TAKEN. FIRE OUT ON ARRIVAL OF CREW.

INCIDENT NO. 30. TIME 2040.

Rear of 27, Bohun Street, Manselton.	Garage.	Complete destruction.

CAUSE OF FIRE – INCENDIARY BOMBS. PUMP/S IN ATTENDANCE:

INCIDENT NO. 31. TIME 2042.

Lisborn Terrace, Treboeth.	Dwelling House.	Extensive.

CAUSE OF FIRE – INCENDIARY BOMBS. PUMP/S IN ATTENDANCE: 1 L.T. (16).

INCIDENT NO. 32. TIME 2131. [sic]

42, Mansel Street.	Dwelling House.	Slight.

CAUSE OF FIRE – INCENDIARY BOMBS. PUMP/S IN ATTENDANCE: 1 L.T. (26).

INCIDENT NO. 33. TIME 2046.

(Fullers, Westbury.	Cabinet Works.	Nil.)
(Brunswick Street.	Dwelling House.	Minor.)

CAUSE OF FIRE – INCENDIARY BOMBS. PUMP/S IN ATTENDANCE: 1 L.T. (49).

INCIDENT NO. 34. TIME 2050.

Cefn Eithen, Glanmor Road, Uplands.	Dwelling House.	Chair, Mat and floorboards burnt.

CAUSE OF FIRE – INCENDIARY BOMBS. PUMP/S IN ATTENDANCE: 1 L.T. (25). FIRE EXTINGUISHED WITH STIRRUP PUMP.

INCIDENT NO. 35. TIME 2050.

Cwmfelin Works.	Steel Works.	Stores gutted.

CAUSE OF FIRE – INCENDIARY BOMBS. PUMP/S IN ATTENDANCE: 1 L.T. (7).

INCIDENT NO. 36. TIME 2052.

Llangyfelach Road, Brynhyfryd.	Dwelling House and Grocer's Stores.	Partly Destroyed.

CAUSE OF FIRE – INCENDIARY BOMBS. PUMP/S IN ATTENDANCE: 1 L.T. (41).

[fo. 6] *Continuation No. 5.*

Premises.	*Description of Premises.*	*Damage Incurred.*
INCIDENT NO. 37. TIME 2054.		
St. Andrew's Church.	Place of Worship.	Damage to rear portion of Church.
Shaftesbury Hall.	Old Cinema.	Damage to part of Shaftesbury Hall.
CAUSE OF FIRE – INCENDIARY BOMBS.	*PUMP/S IN ATTENDANCE: 1 L.T. (23).*	
INCIDENT NO. 38. TIME 2056.		
Waste Ground near Saron Chapel.	Stores – Spare parts etc.	Gutted.
Shed owned by Mr. North (Showman).		
CAUSE OF FIRE – INCENDIARY BOMBS.	*PUMP/S IN ATTENDANCE: 1 L.T. (28).*	
INCIDENT NO. 39. TIME 2057.		
Lon Cothi & Elphin Crescent.	Roadway.	No trace of fire.
CAUSE OF FIRE –	*PUMP/S IN ATTENDANCE: 1 L.T. (30).*	
INCIDENT NO. 40. TIME 2058.		
Recorder Street.	Dwelling House.	Gutted.
CAUSE OF FIRE – INCENDIARY BOMBS.	*PUMP/S IN ATTENDANCE: 1 L.T. (21).*	
INCIDENT NO. 41. TIME 2058.		
Corner of Elphin Crescent & Goronwy Road.	Roadway.	Slight.
CAUSE OF FIRE – HIGH EXPLOSIVE. BOMB ON GAS MAIN.	*PUMP/S IN ATTENDANCE: 1 L.T. (33).*	
INCIDENT NO. 42. TIME 2102.		
47, Sketty Road.	Dwelling House.	Nil.
CAUSE OF FIRE – INCENDIARY BOMB. NO ACTION TAKEN BY CREW. FIRE OUT ON ARRIVAL.	*PUMP/S IN ATTENDANCE: 1 L.T. (50).*	
INCIDENT NO. 43. TIME 2106.		
Paxton Yard, Opposite Goal [*sic*] Main Gate	Timber Yard & Builders' Stores.	Slight.
CAUSE OF FIRE – INCENDIARY BOMBS.	*PUMP/S IN ATTENDANCE: 2 L.T. (40 & 52).*	

[fo. 7] *Continuation No. 6.*

Premises.	*Description of Premises.*	*Damage Incurred.*
INCIDENT NO. 44. TIME 2120.		
Shed near Salem Chapel.	Shed.	Slight.
CAUSE OF FIRE – INCENDIARY BOMB. PUMP/S IN ATTENDANCE: 1 H.T. (B2).		
INCIDENT NO. 45. TIME 2126.		
J. & P. Bevan, Clarence Terrace.	Garage.	No Fire.
CAUSE OF FIRE – NO ACTION TAKEN BY CREW. PUMP/S IN ATTENDANCE: 1 H.T. (35).		
INCIDENT NO. 46. TIME 2141.		
29, Graiglwyd Road.	Roadway.	Gas Main on Fire.
CAUSE OF FIRE – HIGH EXPLOSIVE BOMB. PUMP/S IN ATTENDANCE: 1 L.T. (36).		
INCIDENT NO. 47. TIME 2158.		
Hawthorne Avenue and Sketty Road.	Dwelling House.	Extensive.
CAUSE OF FIRE – HIGH EXPLOSIVE BOMB. PUMP/S IN ATTENDANCE: NO ACTION TAKEN BY CREW.		
INCIDENT NO. 48.	*TIME 2219.*	
28, Carlton Terrace, Swansea.	Dwelling House.	Minor.
CAUSE OF FIRE – INCENDIARY BOMBS. PUMP/S IN ATTENDANCE: 1 L.T. (37).		
INCIDENT NO. 49.	*TIME 2220.*	
Penlan Road.	Dwelling House.	Complete Destruction due to High Explosive.
CAUSE OF FIRE – HIGH EXPLOSIVE BOMB & INCENDIARY BOMBS. PUMP/S IN ATTENDANCE: 2 L.T. (42 & 17).		
INCIDENT NO. 50. TIME 2229.		
Richardson Street, Swansea.	Dwelling House.	House Gutted.
CAUSE OF FIRE – INCENDIARY BOMBS. PUMP/S IN ATTENDANCE: 1 H.T. (A9).		

[fo. 8] *Continuation No. 7.*

Premises	*Description of Premises.*	*Damage Incurred.*
INCIDENT NO. 51. TIME 2307.		
Ffynone Terrace.	Dwelling House.	Building gutted.
CAUSE OF FIRE – INCENDIARY BOMBS.	*PUMP/S IN ATTENDANCE: 1 L.T. (39).*	
INCIDENT NO. 52. TIME 2312.		
Bryn-y-mor Road.	Shop.	Minor.
CAUSE OF FIRE – INCENDIARY BOMBS. *FIRE EXTINGUISHED BY SAND.*	*PUMP/S IN ATTENDANCE: 1 L.T. (48).*	
INCIDENT NO. 53. TIME 2319.		
Court Parade and No's 3 and 30 Gower Road.	Dwelling Houses.	No. 3, Scullery badly burnt. No. 2, Small bedroom and contents badly burnt.
CAUSE OF FIRE – INCENDIARY BOMBS.	*PUMP/S IN ATTENDANCE: 1 L.T. (50).*	
INCIDENT NO. 54. TIME 2319.		
Richardson Street.	Dwelling House.	Extinguished by Regional Crew.
CAUSE OF FIRE – INCENDIARY BOMBS.	*PUMP/S IN ATTENDANCE: 1 L.T. (22).*	
INCIDENT NO. 55. TIME 2320.		
J.H. Morgan's Works, Opposite Sketty Church.	Cabinet Works.	Top Floor partially burnt.
CAUSE OF FIRE – INCENDIARY BOMBS.	*PUMP/S IN ATTENDANCE: 1 L.T. (10).*	
INCIDENT NO. 56. TIME 2322.		
29, Queen's Road, Sketty.	Dwelling House.	One Bedroom burnt out and floor damaged.
CAUSE OF FIRE – INCENDIARY BOMBS.	*PUMP/S IN ATTENDANCE: 1 L.T. (10).*	
INCIDENT NO. 57. TIME 2322.		
Eversley Road, Sketty.	Back Lane behind Eversley Road – G.H. Morgan's Work's Cabinet.	Top Floor partially burnt.
CAUSE OF FIRE – INCENDIARY BOMBS.	*PUMP/S IN ATTENDANCE: 1 L.T. (25).*	
INCIDENT NO. 58. TIME 2324.		
Sketty Ambulance Headquarters.		
FALSE ALARM.	*PUMP/S IN ATTENDANCE: 1 L.T. (40).*	

[fo. 9] *Continuation No. 8.*

Premises.	*Description of Premises.*	*Damage Incurred.*
INCIDENT NO. 59. TIME 2324.		
House Opposite Sketty Police Station.	Dwelling House.	None ascertainable.
CAUSE OF FIRE – INCENDIARY BOMBS.	*PUMP/S IN ATTENDANCE: 1 L.T. (30).*	
INCIDENT NO. 60. TIME 2329.		
Pantgwyn, Sketty Park Road.	Bungalow.	Bathroom burnt.
CAUSE OF FIRE – INCENDIARY BOMBS.	*PUMP/S IN ATTENDANCE: 1 L.T. (36).*	
INCIDENT NO. 61. TIME 2335.		
St. Machan's Lodge, Gower Road.	Dwelling House.	Bedroom burnt.
CAUSE OF FIRE – INCENDIARY BOMB.	*PUMP/S IN ATTENDANCE: 1 L.T. (30).*	
NO ACTION BY CREW. FIRE OUT ON ARRIVAL.		
INCIDENT NO. 62. TIME 0100.		
Alun Road, Mayhill.	Dwelling House.	Wrecked.
CAUSE OF FIRE – INCENDIARY BOMBS. AND HIGH EXPLOSIVE BOMBS.	*PUMP/S IN ATTENDANCE: 1 L.T. (25).*	
INCIDENT NO. 63. TIME 0112.		
50, Manor Road, Manselton.	Dwelling House.	Settee and chair burning.
CAUSE OF FIRE – INCENDIARY BOMBS.	*PUMP/S IN ATTENDANCE: STIRRUP PUMP.*	
INCIDENT NO. 64. TIME 0135.		
Hafod Siding.	Ash Tip.	No trace of fire.
CAUSE OF FIRE –	*PUMP/S IN ATTENDANCE: 1 L.T. (41).*	
INCIDENT NO. 65. TIME		
Lamb Street.		
CAUSE OF FIRE –	*PUMP/S IN ATTENDANCE: 1 L.T. (14).*	
INCIDENT NO. 66. TIME 0144.		
86, Brynhyfryd Square, Brynhyfryd.	Dwelling House.	Extensive damage to house but some furniture saved.
CAUSE OF FIRE – INCENDIARY BOMBS.	*PUMP/S IN ATTENDANCE:*	

o. 10] *Continuation No. 9.*

Premises.	*Description of Premises.*	*Damage Incurred.*
INCIDENT NO. 67. TIME 0512.		
Peters Street, Waun Wen.	Timber yard.	Extensive.
CAUSE OF FIRE – INCENDIARY BOMBS.		*PUMP/S IN ATTENDANCE: 1 L.T. (49).*
INCIDENT NO. 68. TIME 0516.		
Llangyfelach Road, Pentre Estyll.	Dwelling House.	Totally Destroyed.
CAUSE OF FIRE – HIGH EXPLOSIVE BOMB.		*PUMP/S IN ATTENDANCE: 1 L.T. (45).*
INCIDENT NO. 69. TIME 0600.		
1, Emlyn Gardens, Mayhill.	Dwelling House.	House completely demolished.
CAUSE OF FIRE – HIGH EXPLOSIVE BOMB ON GAS MAIN.		*PUMP/S IN ATTENDANCE: 1 L.T. (34).*
INCIDENT NO. 70. TIME 0710.		
Pen-y-Banc, Treboeth, Houses, No's 1, 2, & 3.	Dwelling Houses.	No. 1 Slight. No. 2 Completely gutted. No. 3 Slight.
CAUSE OF FIRE – INCENDIARY BOMBS.		*PUMP/S IN ATTENDANCE: 1 L.T.*
INCIDENT NO. 71. TIME 1515.		
38, Shelley Crescent.	Demolished Dwelling House.	Demolished by High Explosive Bomb.
CAUSE OF FIRE – HIGH EXPLOSIVE.		*PUMP/S IN ATTENDANCE: 1 L.T. (49).*

[fo. 1] *COUNTY BOROUGH OF SWANSEA.*

AUXILIARY FIRE SERVICE.

SUMMARY OF FIRES ATTENDED – ENEMY ACTION 20.2.41.

Premises.	*Description of Premises.*	*Damage Incurred.*
INCIDENT NO. 1 TIME 20.05		
The Quarry, Heathfield.	Quarry.	Nil.
CAUSE OF FIRE: Incendiary Bomb. Extinguished by Wardens before arrival.		*PUMP USED:* 1 L.T. (41).
INCIDENT NO. 2. TIME 20.08		
Rear of Dillwyn Library, Dillwyn St., Swansea.	Stores.	Extensive.
CAUSE OF FIRE: Incendiary Bombs.		*PUMP USED:* 1 L.T. (49)
INCIDENT NO. 3 TIME 20.12		
Tawe Lodge.	Public Institution.	Bedding & Food Store destroyed.
CAUSE OF FIRE: Incendiary Bomb.		*PUMP USED:* 2 L.T. (23 & 10)
INCIDENT NO. 4 TIME 20.15		
80, Middle Rd., Cwmbwrla.	General Dealers' Stores & Dwelling House.	Contents of front bedroom destroyed.
CAUSE OF FIRE: Incendiary Bomb.		*PUMP USED:* 1 L.T. (19)
INCIDENT NO. 5 TIME 20.20		
81, Manor Road, Manselton. Also Nos. 83, 85 & 79.	Dwelling Houses.	Nos. 81 & 83 completely gutted. Nos. 85 & 79 damage slight.
CAUSE OF FIRE: Incendiary Bombs.		*PUMP USED:* 1 H.T. (A.7)
INCIDENT NO. 6 TIME 20.22		
Logan Cottages, Waunarlwydd.	Cottages.	None visible.
		PUMP USED: 2 L.T. (30 & 50)
NO TRACE OF FIRE ON ARRIVAL.		

fo. 2] PREMISES. DESCRIPTION OF PREMISES. DAMAGE INCURRED.

INCIDENT NO. 7 TIME 20.25

110, Manselton Road. Dwelling House. Extensive.

CAUSE OF FIRE: High Explosive Bomb. *PUMP USED:* 1.L.T. (45)

INCIDENT NO. 8 TIME 20.29

Alexandra Terrace, Cwmbwrla. Private Dwelling House. Gutted.

CAUSE OF FIRE: Incendiary Bomb. *PUMP USED:* 1 L.T. (26)

INCIDENT NO. 9 TIME 20.31

53, Gors Avenue. Dwelling House. House gutted.

CAUSE OF FIRE: Direct hit by H.E. Bomb. *PUMP USED:* 1 L.T. (34)

INCIDENT NO. 10 TIME 20.31

107, Gors Avenue. Dwelling House. House gutted on top floor and roof burnt out.

CAUSE OF FIRE: Direct hit by H.E. Bomb. *PUMP USED:* 1 L.T. (34)

Water stopped 5 mins. after pumping. Only small supply available in bomb crater.

INCIDENT NO. 11 TIME 20.32

13, 14, 15 Brooklands Terrace. Dwelling Houses. No. 14 very extensive. Nos. 13 & 15 roof damaged.

CAUSE OF FIRE: Incendiary Bombs. *PUMP USED:* 3 L.T. (40, 30 & 41)

INCIDENT NO. 12 TIME 20.40

St. James' Church. First Aid Post. Minor.

CAUSE OF FIRE: Incendiary Bomb. *PUMP USED:* 1 L.T. (48)

INCIDENT NO. 13 TIME 20.40

Mackworth Terrace. Dwelling House. Negligible.

CAUSE OF FIRE: Incendiary Bomb. *PUMP USED:* 1 L.T. (29)

[fo. 3] *PREMISES.* *DESCRIPTION OF PREMISES.* *DAMAGE INCURRED.*

INCIDENT NO. 14 TIME 20.41

Premises	Description of Premises	Damage Incurred
Cwmbwrla Works.	Tinplate Factory.	One Shed gutted.

CAUSE OF FIRE: Incendiary Bomb. *PUMP USED:* 1 H.T. (A.3)

INCIDENT NO. 15 TIME 20.41

Premises	Description of Premises	Damage Incurred
Paper Supply Shed. (Opposite Cwmbwrla Works).	Stock Shed.	Extensive.

CAUSE OF FIRE: Incendiary Bomb. *PUMP USED:* 1 H.T. (A.3)
4 L.T.s. (48, 49, 28 & 6)

INCIDENT NO. 16 TIME 20.42

Premises	Description of Premises	Damage Incurred
Swansea Baths & Laundry	Laundry.	

CAUSE OF FIRE: Incendiary Bomb. *PUMP USED:* 1 L.T. (39)

INCIDENT NO. 17 TIME 20.44

Premises	Description of Premises	Damage Incurred
Heathfield – Trees & Gorse.	Vacant Ground.	

NO TRACE OF FIRE. *PUMP USED:* 1 L.T. (25)

INCIDENT NO. 18 TIME 20.44

Premises	Description of Premises	Damage Incurred
Catherine Street.	Dwelling House.	Extensive.

CAUSE OF FIRE: Incendiary Bomb. *PUMP USED:* None used.

INCIDENT NO. 19 TIME 20.47

Premises	Description of Premises	Damage Incurred
59, Terrace Road.	Dwelling House.	Bedroom and roof burned.

CAUSE OF FIRE: Incendiary Bomb. *PUMP USED:* 1 L.T. (36)

INCIDENT NO. 20 TIME 20.47

Premises	Description of Premises	Damage Incurred
110, Manselton Road.	Dwelling House.	Extensive.

CAUSE OF FIRE: High Explosive Bomb. *PUMP USED:* 1 L.T. (16)

INCIDENT NO. 21 TIME 20.50

Premises	Description of Premises	Damage Incurred
Sebastopol Street.	Dwelling House.	Negligible.

CAUSE OF FIRE: Incendiary Bomb. *PUMP USED:* 1 L.T. (29)

[fo. 4]

PREMISES.	DESCRIPTION OF PREMISES.	DAMAGE INCURRED.
INCIDENT NO. 22 TIME 20.57		
Junction of Walters Road & Westbury St.	Dwelling House.	Burnt out.
CAUSE OF FIRE: Incendiary Bombs.		*PUMP USED:* 2 L.T. (49 & 37) 1 H.T. (A.5)
INCIDENT NO. 23 TIME 21.00		
South Wales Transport Garage	Omnibus Garage.	Bus burnt out.
CAUSE OF FIRE: Incendiary Bombs.		*PUMP USED:* 1 L.T. (48).
INCIDENT NO. 24 TIME 21.03		
Offices, I.C.I. Works.	Offices.	Not serious.
CAUSE OF FIRE: Incendiary Bombs.		*PUMP USED:* 1 L.T. (17). Mobile Unit.
INCIDENT NO. 25 TIME 21.05		
55, Walter Rd. (should be 51).	Dwelling House.	Attic and roof burnt out.
CAUSE OF FIRE: Incendiary Bomb.		*PUMP USED:* 1 H.T. (B.2). 2 L.T. (48). (30)
INCIDENT NO. 26 TIME 21.13		
108, Manselton Rd.	Private Dwelling House.	Extensive.
CAUSE OF FIRE: High Explosive Bomb.		*PUMP USED:* 1 L.T. (24).
INCIDENT NO. 27 TIME 21.15		
Middle of Manor Rd., Manselton.	Dwelling House.	House gutted.
CAUSE OF FIRE: Incendiary Bomb.		*PUMP USED:* 1 L.T. (18).
INCIDENT NO. 28 TIME 22.06.		
14, Heathfield Rd.	Dwelling House.	House wrecked.
CAUSE OF FIRE: H.E. Bomb causing smouldering wreckage to burn.		*PUMP USED:* 1 L.T. (50)

[fo. 5]

Premises.	*Description of Premises.*	*Damage Incurred.*
INCIDENT NO. 29 TIME 22.19.		
Nr. Burrows Inn (Timber Yard)	Timber Yard	
CAUSE OF FIRE: Incendiary Bomb.		*PUMP USED:* 1 H.T. (A.1)
INCIDENT NO. 30 TIME 22.20		
Road & Rail Wagons Upper Bank.	Wagon Works	Extensive.
CAUSE OF FIRE: Incendiary Bombs.		*PUMP USED:* 1 L.T. (47).
INCIDENT NO. 31 TIME 22.12		
Coaches at Hafod, Near I.C.I. Works.	Passenger Coaches.	Totally destroyed.
CAUSE OF FIRE: Incendiary Bomb.		*PUMP USED:* 1 L.T. (14).
INCIDENT NO. 32 TIME 22.21		
Prince of Wales Dock.	Warehouse.	Gutted.
CAUSE OF FIRE: Incendiary Bomb.		*PUMP USED:* 1 L.T. (5).
INCIDENT NO. 33 TIME 22.25		
9, 10 & 11, Gorse Avenue, Townhill.	Dwelling House.	9 & 11 – roofs and rafters burnt. No. 10 – gutted.
CAUSE OF FIRE: Incendiary Bombs.		*PUMP USED:* 2 L.T. (36 and 4).
INCIDENT NO. 34 TIME 22.35		
Port Tennant Cooperage.	Cooperage.	
CAUSE OF FIRE: Incendiary Bomb. No fire.		*PUMP USED:* 1 L.T. (29).
INCIDENT NO. 35 TIME 22.45		
Sunderland Forge Cable Co., Harrison's Wharf, P of W. Dock.		Gutted.
CAUSE OF FIRE: Incendiary Bomb.		*PUMP USED:* 1 L.T. (29).

[fo. 6]

PREMISES.	*DESCRIPTION OF PREMISES.*	*DAMAGE INCURRED.*
INCIDENT NO. 36 TIME 22.40		
48, Port Tennant Road, and two houses next door.	Dwelling Houses.	Houses demolished by High Explosive.
CAUSE OF FIRE: High Explosive Bomb.		*PUMP USED:* 1 L.T. (44).
INCIDENT NO. 37 TIME 22.40		
3 Houses, Manor Road, Manselton.	Private Dwellings.	2 burnt. 1 extensive.
CAUSE OF FIRE: Incendiary Bombs.		*PUMP USED:* Pontardawe Regional.
INCIDENT NO. 38 TIME 22.45		
St. Joseph's School, Llangyfelach.	Elementary School.	Extensive to top floor.
CAUSE OF FIRE: Incendiary Bombs.		*PUMP USED:* 1 H.T. (2).
INCIDENT NO. 39 TIME 23.01		
129, Port Tennant Road, Pt. Tennant.	Dwelling House.	
NO FIRE ON ARRIVAL.		*PUMP USED:* 1 L.T. (30).
INCIDENT NO. 40 TIME 23.05		
Margaret Street, St. Thomas.	Dwelling House.	Minor.
CAUSE OF FIRE: Incendiary Bombs.		*PUMP USED:* 1 L.T. (37).
INCIDENT NO. 41 TIME 23.07		
81, 83, 85 & 79 Manor Road, Manselton.	Dwelling Houses.	3 houses gutted. Another partially destroyed: No. 79.
CAUSE OF FIRE: Incendiary Bombs.		*PUMP USED:* 1 L.T. (50).
INCIDENT NO. 42 TIME 23.07		
Brynymor Road.	Dwelling House & Shop.	
CAUSE OF FIRE: Incendiary Bomb.		*PUMP USED:* 1 L.T. (10).

[fo. 7]

PREMISES.	*DESCRIPTION OF PREMISES.*	*DAMAGE INCURRED.*
INCIDENT NO. 43 TIME 23.07		
233, Neath Road, Landore.	Dwelling House.	Extensive.
CAUSE OF FIRE: High Explosive Bomb.		*PUMP USED:* 1 L.T. ( )
INCIDENT NO. 44 TIME 23.09		
Teilo Road, Mayhill.	Dwelling Houses.	Very extensive in the vicinity.
CAUSE OF FIRE: High Explosive Bombs and Incendiaries.		*PUMP USED:* 1 H.T. (A.6).
INCIDENT NO. 45 TIME 23.24		
Gas Main, Town Hill Rd., Mayhill (Near Teilo Road).	Gas Main.	Extensive to Gas Main.
CAUSE OF FIRE: High Explosive Bomb.		*PUMP USED:* 1 L.T. (20).
INCIDENT NO. 46 TIME 24.00		
Oxford Street, Swansea.	Shop.	Buildings demolished.
CAUSE OF FIRE: High Explosive and Incendiary Bombs.		*PUMPS USED:* 1 H.T. (D.3) 2 L.T. (21 &)
INCIDENT NO. 47 TIME 01.12		
Creidiol Road, Mayhill.	Dwelling House.	Two Houses burnt out.
CAUSE OF FIRE: Incendiary Bombs.		*PUMP USED:* 1 L.T. (10).
INCIDENT NO. 48 TIME 01.30		
St. Helens Road, Swansea.	Dwelling House.	Back Portion of house.
CAUSE OF FIRE: Incendiary Bombs.		*PUMP USED:* 1 H.T. (A.9).
INCIDENT NO. 49 TIME 02.05.		
1, Emlyn Gardens, Mayhill.	Dwelling House.	
CAUSE OF FIRE: Direct hit with H.E. Debris on fire.		*PUMP USED:* 1 L.T. (34).

[fo. 8]

PREMISES.	*DESCRIPTION OF PREMISES.*	*DAMAGE INCURRED.*
INCIDENT NO. 50 TIME 05.03		
Penygraig Road.	Dwelling House.	
NOT REQUIRED.		*PUMP USED:* 1 H.T. (3.5).
INCIDENT NO. 51 TIME 05.59		
24, Courtney Street (Renew damping down).	Dwelling House.	
CAUSE OF FIRE: Incendiary Bomb.		*PUMP USED:* 1 L.T. (38).
INCIDENT NO. 52 TIME 06.55		
Port Tennant Rd.	Dwelling House.	Slight. (Bed burnt).
CAUSE OF FIRE: Incendiary Bomb.		*PUMP USED:* 1 L.T. (29).

[fo. 1] *COUNTY BOROUGH OF SWANSEA.*

AUXILIARY FIRE SERVICE.

SUMMARY OF FIRES ATTENDED – ENEMY ACTION 21.2.41/22.2.41.

Premises.	*Description of Premises.*	*Damage Incurred.*
INCIDENT NO. 1. TIME 1845.		
Hendrefoilan Farm, Dunvant.	Hay ricks.	Extensive.
CAUSE OF FIRE:– INCENDIARY BOMBS. PUMP/S IN ATTENDANCE:– 1 L.T. (30).		
INCIDENT NO. 2. TIME 1950.		
Dean's Shop.	Grocer's Shop.	Slight.
14, Careg Gardens.	Dwelling House.	Property gutted, but adjoining property saved.
CAUSE OF FIRE:– INCENDIARY BOMBS. PUMP/S IN ATTENDANCE:– STIRRUP PUMP.		
INCIDENT NO. 3. TIME 2035.		
Swansea Hospital, St. Helen's Road.	Hospital.	Extensive.
CAUSE OF FIRE:– INCENDIARY BOMBS. PUMP/S IN ATTENDANCE:– 1 L.T. (48).		
INCIDENT NO. 4. TIME 2035.		
Tenby Hotel.	Public House.	Extensive.
CAUSE OF FIRE:– INCENDIARY BOMBS. PUMP/S IN ATTENDANCE:– 1 H.T.(A5.)		
INCIDENT NO. 5. TIME 2038.		
St. Helen's Avenue.	Dwelling House.	No Fire Discernible.
CAUSE OF FIRE:– PUMP/S IN ATTENDANCE:– 1 L.T. (37).		
INCIDENT NO. 6. TIME 2044.		
33, Carlton Terrace.	Dwelling House.	Slight.
CAUSE OF FIR: – INCENDIARY BOMBS. PUMP/S IN ATTENDANCE:– 1 L.T. (41).		
INCIDENT NO. 7. TIME 2045.		
Hanover Street.	Dwelling House.	Slight.
CAUSE OF FIRE:– INCENDIARY BOMBS. PUMP/S IN ATTENDANCE:– 1 L.T. (30).		
INCIDENT NO. 8. TIME 2045.		
Girl's High School, Walter Road.	High School.	Not extensive.
CAUSE OF FIRE:– INCENDIARY BOMBS. PUMP/S IN ATTENDANCE:– 1 L.T.(25).		

[fo. 2] *Continuation No. 1.*

Premises.	*Description of Premises.*	*Damage Incurred.*

INCIDENT NO. 9. TIME 2054.

Tyrhester Farm, Cockett.	Farm Dwelling, Hay Rick afire.	Two Hay Ricks burnt.

CAUSE OF FIRE – INCENDIARY BOMBS. PUMP/S IN ATTENDANCE:– 1 L.T. (28).

INCIDENT NO. 10. TIME 2045.

Victoria Avenue.	Dwelling House.	Extensive.

CAUSE OF FIRE – INCENDIARY BOMBS. PUMP/S IN ATTENDANCE:– STIRRUP PUMP.

INCIDENT NO. 11. TIME 2050.

Phillip's Parade.	Dwelling House.	Gutted and Demolished.

CAUSE OF FIRE:– INCENDIARY BOMBS. PUMP/S IN ATTENDANCE:– 1 L.T. (37).

INCIDENT NO. 12. TIME 2051.

Cavendish Furnishers, Ltd.,	Furniture Stores.	Gutted.

CAUSE OF FIRE:– INCENDIARY BOMBS. PUMP/S IN ATTENDANCE:– 1 H.T. (S5).

INCIDENT NO. 13. TIME 2052.

Leslie's Stores, High Street.	Department Stores.	No Fire.

NO FIRE AT LESLIE'S STORES – SEVERAL FIRES IN VICINITY WHICH CREW ASSISTED IN DEALING WITH.

CAUSE OF FIRE:– INCENDIARY BOMBS. PUMP/S IN ATTENDANCE:–

INCIDENT NO. 14. TIME 2054.

Boots Cash Chemists, Oxford Street.	Shop. (Chemist's).	Burnt out.

CAUSE OF FIRE:– INCENDIARY BOMBS. PUMP/S IN ATTENDANCE:– 1 L.T. (38).

INCIDENT NO. 15. TIME 2055.

Belgrave Court, Walter Road.	Flats.	Slight.

CAUSE OF FIRE – INCENDIARY BOMBS. PUMP/S IN ATTENDANCE:– STIRRUP PUMP.

INCIDENT NO. 16. TIME 2055.

47, Pantycelyn Road.	Dwelling House.	Top floor and Furniture burnt.

CAUSE OF FIRE – INCENDIARY BOMBS. PUMP/S IN ATTENDANCE:– 1 L.T. (34).

[fo. 3] *Continuation No. 2.*

Premises.	*Description of Premises.*	*Damage Incurred.*
INCIDENT NO. 17. TIME 2055.		
3, Pantycelyn Road.	Dwelling House.	Burnt Out.
CAUSE OF FIRE:– INCENDIARY BOMBS. PUMP/S IN ATTENDANCE:– 1 L.T. (34).		
INCIDENT NO. 18. TIME 2057.		
Victoria Road, Waunarlwydd.	Dwelling House.	Fire extinguished by householders fire party.
CAUSE OF FIRE:– INCENDIARY BOMB. PUMP/S IN ATTENDANCE:– 1 L.T. (20).		
INCIDENT NO. 19. TIME 2057.		
County Court Buildings, St. Mary's Square.	Offices.	Extensive.
CAUSE OF FIRE:– INCENDIARY BOMBS. PUMP/S IN ATTENDANCE:– 1 L.T. (24).		
INCIDENT NO. 20. TIME 2059.		
Ivor L. Roberts, De-La-Beche St.	Garages.	Slight.
CAUSE OF FIRE:– INCENDIARY BOMBS. PUMP/S IN ATTENDANCE:– 1 L.T. (17).		
INCIDENT NO. 21. TIME 2100.		
Brynymor Road District – Kensington Crescent.	Dwelling House.	Extensive.
CAUSE OF FIRE:– INCENDIARY BOMBS. PUMP/S IN ATTENDANCE: 1 L.T. (47).		
INCIDENT NO. 22. TIME 2100.		
B.B.C. Studios	Broadcasting Studios.	) Completely Destroyed.
Trinity Church.	Place of Worship.	)
British Home Stores.	Department Stores.	)
Waterloo Street.	Offices, houses, etc..	)
Belle Vue Street.	Houses, etc.	) Extensive.
Dynevor Place.	Dynevor Schools, etc.	)
Albert Hall.	Picture House.	)
Treseder's Stores.	Oil Stores.	)
CAUSE OF FIRE:– INCENDIARY BOMBS. PUMP/S IN ATTENDANCE:– 3 L.T. (16, 17, 19). 2 H.T. (S.4, S.2).		

[fo. 4] *Continuation No. 3.*

Premises.	*Description of Premises.*	*Damage Incurred.*
INCIDENT NO. 23. TIME 2100.		
Church Road, Llansamlet.	Dwelling House.	Slight.
CAUSE OF FIRE:– INCENDIARY BOMBS. PUMP/S IN ATTENDANCE:– STIRRUP PUMP.		
INCIDENT NO. 24. TIME 2102.		
Oxford Street, Nr. Portland Street.	Shops, Offices, etc.	Extensive.
CAUSE OF FIRE:– INCENDIARY BOMBS. PUMP/S IN ATTENDANCE:– 1 L.T. (45).		
INCIDENT NO. 25. TIME 2102.		
10, Duke Street,	Dwelling House.	Slight.
Duke's Garage.	Garage.	Slight.
CAUSE OF FIRE:– INCENDIARY BOMBS. PUMP/S IN ATTENDANCE:– 1 L.T. (14).		
INCIDENT NO. 26. TIME 2105.		
192, 193 and 194, Kensington Crescent.	Dwelling Houses.	Two Burnt Out.
CAUSE OF FIRE:– INCENDIARY BOMBS. PUMP/S IN ATTENDANCE:– 1 L.T. (A9).		
INCIDENT NO. 27. TIME 2105.		
Parish Church, Llansamlet.	Place of Worship.	Slight.
CAUSE OF FIRE:– INCENDIARY BOMBS. PUMP/S IN ATTENDANCE:– STIRRUP PUMP.		
INCIDENT NO. 28. TIME 2107.		
Weaver's, North Dock.	Flour Mills.	Slight.
CAUSE OF FIRE:– INCENDIARY BOMBS. PUMP/S IN ATTENDANCE:– 1 H.T. (S2).		
INCIDENT NO. 29. TIME 2109.		
11, De-la-beche St.	Offices, etc.	Extensive.
CAUSE OF FIRE:– INCENDIARY BOMBS. PUMP/S IN ATTENDANCE:– 1 L.T. (52).		
INCIDENT NO. 30. TIME 2111.		
Windsor Street.		Slight.
CAUSE OF FIRE:– INCENDIARY BOMBS. PUMP/S IN ATTENDANCE:– 1 L.T. (15).		
INCIDENT NO. 31. TIME 2115.		
12, Bond Street.	Dwelling House.	Extensive.
CAUSE OF FIRE:– INCENDIARY BOMBS. PUMP/S IN ATTENDANCE:– 1 L.T. (39).		

[fo. 5] *Continuation No. 4.*

Premises.	*Description of Premises.*	*Damage Incurred.*
INCIDENT NO. 32. TIME 2120.		
Elementary School, Llansamlet.	School.	Slight.
CAUSE OF FIRE:– INCENDIARY BOMBS. PUMP/S IN ATTENDANCE:– STIRRUP PUMP.		
INCIDENT NO. 33. TIME 2127.		
3, Brunswick Street, Swansea.	Dwelling House.	Slight.
CAUSE OF FIRE:– INCENDIARY BOMBS. PUMP/S IN ATTENDANCE:– 1 L.T. (21).		
INCIDENT NO. 34. TIME 2133.		
Merriman & Stephens, South Dock.	Coal Yard.	Slight.
CAUSE OF FIRE:– INCENDIARY BOMBS. PUMP/S IN ATTENDANCE:– 1 L.T. (6).		
INCIDENT NO. 35. TIME 2150.		
Rutland Street School.	School and Food Controller's Offices, etc.	Building Burnt Out.
CAUSE OF FIRE:– INCENDIARY BOMBS. PUMP/S IN ATTENDANCE: 1 L.T. (44).		
VARIOUS OTHER FIRES WERE ALSO DEALT WITH IN THE VICINITY OF ST. MARY'S CHURCH.		
INCIDENT NO. 36. TIME 2153.		
Market, Oxford St.	Market.	Burnt Out.
CAUSE OF FIRE:– INCENDIARY BOMBS. PUMP/S IN ATTENDANCE: 1 L.T. (10).		
INCIDENT NO. 37. TIME 2223.		
Picture House and Adjacent Buildings.	Picture House.	Burnt Out.
CAUSE OF FIRE:– INCENDIARY BOMBS. PUMP/S IN ATTENDANCE: 1 L.T. (18).		
INCIDENT NO. 38. TIME 2250.		
4, Brooklands Terrace.	Dwelling House.	Gutted.
CAUSE OF FIRE:– INCENDIARY BOMBS. PUMP/S IN ATTENDANCE:– 1 H.T. (A6).		
INCIDENT NO. 39. TIME 2250.		
5, Brooklands Terrace.	Dwelling House.	Top Floor and Roof Damaged.
CAUSE OF FIRE:– INCENDIARY BOMBS. PUMP/S IN ATTENDANCE:– 1 H.T. (A6).		

[fo. 6] *Continuation No. 5.*

Premises.	*Description of Premises.*	*Damage Incurred.*
INCIDENT NO. 40. TIME 2259.		
St. James' Church, Walter Road.	Place of Worship.	Very Slight.
CAUSE OF FIRE:– INCENDIARY BOMBS. PUMP/S IN ATTENDANCE:– 1 L.T. (10).		
INCIDENT NO. 41. TIME 2300.		
Clarence Terrace.	Stores.	Burnt Out.
CAUSE OF FIRE:– INCENDIARY BOMBS. PUMP/S IN ATTENDANCE:– 1 L.T. (30).		
INCIDENT NO. 42. TIME 2305.		
Assembly Rooms, St. Helen's Road.	Tailor's Cutting Shop.	Extensive.
CAUSE OF FIRE:– INCENDIARY BOMBS. PUMP/S IN ATTENDANCE:– 1 L.T. (48).		
INCIDENT NO. 43. TIME 2342.		
Trallwn Road, Llansamlet.		Slight.
CAUSE OF FIRE:– INCENDIARY BOMBS. PUMP/S IN ATTENDANCE:– 1 L.T. (45).		
INCIDENT NO. 44. TIME 0037.		
21/22, Glanbrydan Avenue and 5, Brynmill Crescent.	Dwelling Houses.	No Fires at Addresses given on arrival.
CAUSE OF FIRE:– PUMP/S IN ATTENDANCE:– 1 L.T. (25).		
INCIDENT NO. 45. TIME 0215.		
Wassail Square.	Old Rutland St. School.	Extensive.
CAUSE OF FIRE – INCENDIARY BOMBS. PUMP/S IN ATTENDANCE: 1 H.T. (B2).		
INCIDENT NO. 46. TIME 0325.		
Northampton Lane, Nr. Electricity Sub Station.	Dwelling House.	Extensive.
CAUSE OF FIRE:– INCENDIARY BOMBS. PUMP/S IN ATTENDANCE:– 1 L.T. (25).		
INCIDENT NO. 47. TIME 0335.		
Kensington Crescent.	Dwelling House.	House Demolished.
CAUSE OF FIRE:– INCENDIARY BOMBS. PUMP/S IN ATTENDANCE:– 1 L.T. (37).		
INCIDENT NO. 48. TIME 0555.		
William Bros., Heathfield Street.	Ironmongers.	Extensive.
CAUSE OF FIRE:– INCENDIARY BOMBS. PUMP/S IN ATTENDANCE:– 1 L.T. (50).		

[fo. 7] *Continuation No. 6.*

REMARKS:–

There are premises destroyed by fire and other Incidents which occurred on this particular night, which are not included in the Summary, because no Fire Reports have come in from the Stations to cover them, due to the fact that, Crews and Units were being turned out (particularly in the case of Fisher Street Auxiliary Fire Station), and going from one job to another, very often linking up with other Units and Crews in efforts to stem the spreading of the fires. Nevertheless, reports given are the recorded number of calls to Fires, which were transmitted from Central Control or the usual sources, and sent in by the Stations in the usual way.

Document 4: Select Press Reports on the 'Three Nights' Blitz' (Swansea City Archives Office, D.6 (Local Newspapers)).

A) South Wales Evening Post, Thursday, 20 February 1941.

[p. 1]

HEAVY NIGHT RAID ON SWANSEA

Loss Of Life Reported In Attack Lasting Some Hours

FIRE BOMB FIGHTERS' FINE WORK

R.A.F. Night Planes Challenge the Bombers

Swansea was heavily attacked by Nazi raiders last night [19 February]. A number of people were killed and damage was done to a considerable number of houses and business premises.

The raid lasted some hours, and incendiaries and high explosive bombs were dropped. Magnificent work was done by the fire-fighting services and by the general public in grappling with the incendiaries showered on the town and in dealing with the fires.

The incendiaries started a series of fires over a wide area, but these were attacked with such speed and efficiency that they were prevented from developing into big outbreaks.

In fact, later arrivals among the raiders could find little to guide them. Harassed by R.A.F. night fighters who went up to challenge them, they appeared to drop their bombs indiscriminately.

MINISTRY COMMUNIQUE

An Air Ministry and Ministry of Home Security communique stated this morning:

"During the early hours of last night enemy air-craft made an attack on a town in South Wales.

"High explosive bombs caused damage to a considerable number of houses and business premises, but incendiary bombs were dealt with very promptly.

"None of the fires caused was serious, and all had been put out by an early hour this morning.

"Casualties included a number of people killed.

"A short attack was made on the London area, where some damage was caused. The number of casualties was small, very few people being killed."

[The remainder of this communiqué and of the very long article which followed was devoted exclusively to raids on London and the Home Counties.]

B) South Wales Evening Post, Friday, 21 February 1941.

[p. 1]

MURDER RAIDERS AGAIN BLITZ SWANSEA

Town Valiantly Faces Another Night Ordeal

60–70 H.E. BOMBS IN LONG ATTACK

NAZI MURDER RAIDERS AGAIN CONCENTRATED THEIR ATTENTION LAST NIGHT [20 February] ON SWANSEA, AND CONSIDERABLE DAMAGE TO PROPERTY AND DEATH AND INJURY RESULTED FROM A HEAVY ATTACK.

The bombers visited several areas in South Wales, Swansea was made the main target, and was attacked by steady streams of raiders for several hours.

The raid began with the usual flares, followed by showers of incendiaries, some of the explosive type, and then by between 60 and 70 high explosive bombs.

There was intense gunfire, which kept the raiders flying high. Fires were started, but magnificent work by the fire-fighting services and by fire-watchers prevented the development of any serious blaze.

Considerable damage was done to commercial buildings and houses, and there were a number of casualties, including some people killed.

An A.R.P. warden was killed when a high explosive bomb fell near him in a main street, and a part-time worker also lost his life. Ten people were injured when another bomb struck an A.F.S. post.

[p. 4]

SWANSEA'S NIGHT BATTLE WITH INCENDIARIES

CIVILIAN ARMY SANDBAGGED FIRE BOMBS

From the medley of confused impressions made by the raid on Swansea on Wednesday night [19 February], one emerges clearly and proudly — the courage and promptitude with which the residents sprang to the attack on the countless fire bombs.

Wherever an incendiary fell a man, woman or boy sprang from cover with poised sandbag and smothered the bomb almost as soon as it burst into flame.

The number of casualties is not definitely announced.

The medical services had to make a quick change over from the normal organisation for dealing with casualties at a hospital when a bomb struck the casualty department, causing many deaths.

Immediately other hospitals in the town and one in an adjacent area were brought into commission to deal with many injured, and the ambulance services worked smoothly in spite of this early handicap.

RESCUE MEN KILLED

Among the dead are two rescue workers who were killed by blast when a bomb, one of a stick of four, which did considerable damage near a large block of residential flats, totally destroying a house on the opposite side of the street.

SUCCESSION OF PLANES

The raid started with the arrival of a few planes, followed by a succession of others, which strewed incendiaries.

These must have numbered thousands. Groups of scores of them could be seen alight, and then almost at once their numbers were thinned as they were tackled by fire personnel, civilians, or as they burnt themselves out on open ground.

Indeed, the first impression of the raid was the almost miraculous disappearance of these incendiaries.

This impression was fully justified, when, at the end of a visitation lasting some hours, there was no outstanding fire to be recorded, and comparative little damage from fire anywhere. In the streets and on open spaces, when daylight came, there were to be seen hundreds of sandy heaps where bombs had been extinguished.

HIGH EXPLOSIVES

The effect of the high explosives which followed the incendiaries was very different. The bombs were widely distributed, and although these were apparently not of the highest calibre, the damage is of a very widespread character.

Several areas were evacuated in consequence of either explosions of *[sic]* time bombs.

One of the features of the raid was the number of important buildings which had narrow escapes.

A Methodist chapel was badly damaged.

NURSES FIGHT FIRE BOMBS

A time bomb dropped on land adjacent to a Methodist chapel in one of the suburbs, and evacuation was necessary from the district.

In one hospital nurses successfully dealt with incendiary bombs.

In one cinema in the town an incendiary came through the roof and fell back stage. Sparks were visible to the audience, but perfect order prevailed.

A number of staff rushed to deal with the bomb, and while the manager was announcing, "It is only an incendiary bomb" a loud bang caused him to correct himself and add "– of an explosive type".

The effect of the bomb was to disable the loud speakers temporarily and the performance could not proceed, although half the audience remained.

There were many instances of staffs being told to report to temporary offices, because of their shops and offices being evacuated.

In one area the father of the household, who was suffering from pneumonia, was carried downstairs to safety, but a bomb fell and destroyed the house, killing several members of the family.

Members of the A.R.P. personnel were attracted by a man fighting an incendiary in a front garden. The man said: "This is all right. Attend to that one over there" indicating a house where smoek *[sic]* was issuing from the roof.

The A.R.P. workers found an incendiary burning in the loft of the house, and they had to approach it through the trap door, using the door as a shield.

They extinguished the fire bombs and were amazed afterwards to find that, unknown to them, it had been burning in the house of the man in the garden.

More than a dozen incendiaries fell on a playing field. They were seen by many householders on fire-watching duty, and men could be plainly seen darting through the "blobs" of fire, carrying sand-bags, which they dumped on the bombs, extinguishing them immediately.

FLARES OVER SEA

Less than a hundred yards away, another batch of incendiaries landed on open space surrounded by trees, and one or two wooden seats caught fire.

Later, many flares were dropped over the sea, and the parachutes were plainly visible as targets for tracer bullets.

In one district where many bombs were dropped, a family of six was trapped in the cellar of their house. Rescue workers were immediately on the scene, and worked furiously when it became known that water was flooding the cellar.

HOUSING EVACUATED PEOPLE

In one area a bomb split a house in two, and three residents in the undamaged half were safe.

Several Church Halls and Schools were used to house evacuated people.

Two men reported to the police station that they were due to report to-day as recruits at a military unit some distance away. Their house had been bombed and their documents and warrants destroyed.

A number of calls were made upon the fire brigade in cases where the attacks got beyond the control of the fire-fighting parties in the locality.

One of the strangest incidents of the raid occurred in a big office.

An oil bomb struck the roof of a big block and brushed passed a man sitting at his desk making a huge hole in the floor near his chair. A rush of wind upset the man's balance and fell through the hole in the floor.

He was practically unhurt as he scrambled to his feet on the floor below, just as flames began to come from the bomb.

SAND BAG WAR SUCCESS

By yesterday afternoon when admirable progress had been made with clearance works and with first-aid repairs. First impressions that the civilians' helping in attacking incendiaries had been of the most praise-worthy character were confirmed.

There were conclusive pieces of evidence. First there was the rarity of burnt-out premises among the damaged buildings.

Only ten of the outbreaks became even minor fires and the sand bag war and the fire bombs was followed by work as devoted and expeditious by the fire services on small fires.

The amateur and trained fire-fighters deserved well of their fellow citizens. They and the police escaped with only minor injuries, but two rescue workers and a warden lost their lives.

One feature of the raid was the ill-luck of some residents in having a second visitation from the bombers.

A large proportion of the damage is in residential streets.

Several bombs which fell in the radius of a few streets in one residential district, caused a great deal of damage, but surprisingly few casualties.

DOCTOR'S HOUSE DAMAGED

Many houses received direct hits, and one of these was attached to a doctor's house. The occupiers ran into the doctor's home, which was damaged by blast and showers of slates and stones, and there they remained for the rest of the night.

A housewife in another district acted as shelter hostess to a number of women neighbours who were out fire-watching. She made them comfortable in her garden shelter, and stood in the doorway armed with a stirrup pump, ready for any emergency. Later she soothed some frightened children and used up most of her rations in preparing a meal for her neighbours.

BRANCH POST OFFICE

A branch post office and a branch bank office in perhaps the most severely damaged street was struck, and a cafe which had been empty for some time was destroyed by a bomb.

In many of the streets affected, householders stood outside their damaged homes arranging articles of furniture they had managed to salvage. Demolition workers were busy in many areas, and windows broken by blast and shrapnel received prompt attention.

TIME-BOMB TRAGEDY

Further tragedy came to one district when a time bomb exploded during the lunch-hour. A street in which it had landed had been barricaded, and was guarded by police officers, but three little boys are believed to have lost their lives when the explosion occurred.

A person living in the area told a reporter: "The policemen had asked the little boys to go away several times, and had warned older people loitering about that the danger was imminent. The boys had apparently eluded the police officers and were near the dangerous house when the bomb went off".

Barricades were erected in a neighbourhood where another time-bomb was discovered.

HOSPITAL DAMAGE

The secretary-superintendent of a hospital told a reporter that a number of incendiaries fell on the building, and these were promptly dealt with. A high explosive bomb which fell near damaged the casualty department and broke windows in the operating theatre and one side of the building. The electricity supply was interfered with. The patients had been previously removed from the basement, and the superintendent said that they stood the ordeal courageously.

A number of people who were in wards where the windows were broken were subsequently transferred to another hospital.

C) South Wales Evening Post, Saturday 22 February 1941.

[p. 1]

SWANSEA AGAIN: SEVERE DAMAGE IN TOWN'S THIRD NIGHT ORDEAL

Waves of Raiders Shower Fire Bombs and High Explosives

Churches, Business Premises and Houses Suffer

SWANSEA, FOR THE THIRD NIGHT IN SUCCESSION [21 February], WAS THE MAIN TARGET FOR THE NAZI RAIDERS, WHO RAINED HIGH-EXPLOSIVE AND FIRE BOMBS ON THE TOWN CAUSING SEVERE DAMAGE AND A NUMBER OF CASUALTIES, SOME FATAL.

As on the two previous nights, a stream of raiders scattered fire bombs indiscriminately, and then, while members of the civil defence services were working at top speed dealing with the incendiaries, high explosives crashed down.

Later came more showers of fire bombs and watchers again performed heroically in helping to render them harmless.

Among the places damaged were churches, houses and shops, schools, a market and a chapel.

GERMAN VERSION

The German news agency account of the raid broadcast this morning stated:

"Swansea was again the target of German air attack last night.

"This is the third night in succession that Swansea has been bombed.

"Several large and small fires were observed, and there were some explosions.

"British anti-aircraft fire was again only slight."

Other places in South Wales received alerts, but no reports of any incidents have been received.

MINISTRY STATEMENT

An Air Ministry and Ministry of Home Security communique issued early to-day said:

"During the early part of the night enemy aircraft attacked a town in South Wales.

"High explosives and incendiary bombs were dropped in this attack, which lasted for about three and a half hours.

"Fires were started, and damage was done to houses and business premises.

"There was a number of casualties, including some persons killed.

"There was also some activity over Eastern England for a short period during the night.

"A few bombs were dropped, some of them in the London area. No great damage was done and casualties were few."

The bodies of two people, husband and wife, were extricated from a demolished house in one London district. They had been buried under piles of wreckage when their home, a semi-detached house, was hit by a high explosive.

A rescue party worked for more than eight hours during the night in the hope of getting them out alive.

[p.4]

SWANSEA'S THURSDAY NIGHT RAID

Thursday night's [20 February] attack on Swansea, which began after nightfall followed the usual blitz technique, the raining down of incendiaries, the use of parachute flares, and then the arrival of relays of raiders with high-explosive bombs.

Thursday night's bombing, however, was more severe than on the previous night, it being apparent that the bombs included some of heavy calibre.

It is feared that the casualty list may be greater than on Wednesday night.

In one road on a housing estate an entire row of houses was burned in spite of the heroic efforts of the A.F.S.

WARDEN KILLED

There were some casualties among the civil defence services. A warden was killed when a high explosive bomb dropped near him in a business street, damaging shops and offices and narrowly missing a chapel. A part-time A.F.S. man died from injuries received when fighting a blaze. A direct hit was made by a high explosive bomb on an A.F.S. Station. A number of men were injured.

HOUSES SUFFERED MOST

Damage was principally to house property, although in some areas, the falling of bombs at spots affected in the raid on the previous night caused more streets to be closed to traffic.

Bus services were quickly adjusted to the new conditions.

Hundreds of people are being cared for at rest centres in various parts of the town.

A school was damaged by fire, and a large crater now exists where a big suburban bakery was in operation.

People in one house were unhurt when a bomb fell and demolished brick garages recently erected at the rear of the house. This bomb wrecked windows over a wide area, before it burst in face of terraces of houses.

A large grocer's shop which had its windows blown out on Wednesday, and which had been temporarily barricaded on Thursday, was involved in a fire on Thursday night, and an incendiary caused a slight outbreak as *[sic]* the ruins of a house nearby which had been struck by a high explosive bomb less than 24 hours before.

Rescue parties were busy all through the night in bringing people out of wrecked houses.

D) South Wales Evening Post, Monday, 24 February 1941.

[p. 1]

INJURED WOMEN AND CHILDREN AMONG SWANSEA'S HEROES

Doctor's Tribute To "Most Amazing Courage"

HEROISM OF DEFENCE WORKERS

Trapped Men Found Alive After 24 Hours

WRECKED BUILDINGS TO BE DYNAMITED

AFTER A WEEK-END OF REFLECTION ON THE TRIPLE RAID ON SWANSEA ONE OUTSTANDING IMPRESSION LEFT ON THE MINDS OF THOSE WHO SAW THEM AT WORK WAS OF THE HEROISM AND DEVOTION TO DUTY OF THE WHOLE OF THE DEFENCE SERVICES.

The third night of the blitz found them braving the bombs and fire of the severest of the three attacks, weary, haggard but grimly determined to see it through.

Another impression, recorded in the mind of a doctor who was on duty throughout at a hospital, was of the amazing courage and patience of the injured — men, women and children. In a moving tribute, he said that these brave people upset all pre-conceived ideas of what might be expected from a civil population passing through such an ordeal.

Rescue workers had an encouraging result late on Saturday night in the finding of two trapped men alive in the basement of an office block. They continued fully at work on Sunday upon wrecked premises upon which the attack was mainly felt.

Other bodies found included three under the wreckage of hotels, and among the rescue workers was a man who recognised the bodies of men who were acquaintances of his. Men of the other services were in operation. Streets were being cleared.

Ruins to be Dynamited

Bakers, of whom many were making domestic deliveries, and many of the grocers were at work. Food control officials were making arrangements for wholesalers and retailers for supplies. Many ways in which the forces came to the assistance of the local organisations were in the provision of despatch riders, replenishing the streets and supplies upon which such demands were made during the fire-bomb attack. Walls of some buildings are in a precarious state, and it is understood that dynamiting of these is to begin at once.

The mobile units of various voluntary organisations which have been of greatly appreciated service, included an R.S.P.C.A. ambulance, to collect animals found wandering wild.

The full extent of the casualties is not yet known, but thought to be less than might have been expected from the intensity of the attack.

The injured included one of the town's best known figures, Charlie Evans, newsagent, who has lost a limb.

A sister tutor at one of the hospitals is also among the patients.

Tribute to Injured

A well-known doctor paid a very moving tribute to the dauntless bravery of the injured, whom he had been in contact with during three days at each of the emergency hospitals which took a substantial number of patients when one hospital was hit.

He said the most amazing courage was common to the men, women and children.

"In the days before the war we imagined that under conditions of such great strain there would be groups of frightened people trying to get to hospital, having nothing much the matter with them except fright and nervousness. Exactly the opposite has been the case.

"I saw only two cases whom I really thought were nervousness. One had quite sufficient cause for his nerves, and the other was drunk.

"Even with severe injuries the patients simply lay in bed smiled, spoke quite patiently, and were content to wait until their turn came for attention.

[p. 4]

"These were men, women and children, and there was hardly a whimper even from the youngest child".

The doctor praised the work of the resident surgeons and local surgeons who worked the whole night, and mentioned that there was also a mobile X-ray apparatus on duty.

Food Supplies

The food control office announced that persons whose rations documents had been destroyed, or whose retailers are out of business, should apply for emergency ration cards.

National dried milk for infants can also be obtained by permit.

Many of the food shops remained open on Sunday and several wholesale grocery establishments also kept their premises open to replenish supplies to retailers. Retail grocers needing immediate supplies must consult either the wholesale houses or the food office.

The work of the local bakers was described as strenuous and good. Local resources are augmented by the area board officer.

Officers from the Divisional Food Office rendered valuable assistance from the start of the emergency.

SWANSEA'S PREPARATIONS

The three-day attack imposed a tremendous strain on the civil defence services, but it is a tribute to Swansea's preparations that the municipal machinery was able to function as well as it did.

Of course, there were dislocations, but there was never a complete breakdown of any of the organisations. Men and women who had been on unceasing duty for three days and nights were still carrying on.

The food problem threatened at one time to create a serious situation, but Government departments readily went to the aid of the local authority so as to make distributions as smooth as possible. All the relief services were quickly mobilised and the food situation was handled effectively.

VOLUNTARY EVACUATION

Several mobile canteens called to the town and supplied the people with the necessary food, while large stocks were taken to various centres where the homeless had been accommodated.

Here food was cooked and served by members of the W.V.S., while bedding was provided by the American Red Cross.

The voluntary evacuation of many of the people placed considerable pressure on transport.

But there was a trek to surrounding districts by people who were badly in need of rest.

[p. 3]

SEAS OF FIRE IN SWANSEA RAID

Spotter's Story Of Third Night Of Big Blitz (by GEORGE LONG)

Tumultuous seas of fire and great smoke clouds which threw back a red glow and accompanied by a terrific roar of flame was the last impression I had of the town after being driven from my post of fire-watcher in Swansea on Friday night.

It had been a terrific night, with dive-bombing which obviously directed on the nearby fires in the early stages. It became intensive as the night grew older.

Occasionally, the sound of women's and children's voices could be heard as wardens directed them from shelters which were threatened by the flames.

I saw one such party being brought from a back street in the region of the parish church. It was like daylight in the glare of the flames as they were hurried through debris to another shelter.

Less than half an hour later they were hurried out of this basement to another spot as the building above them had caught fire.

The raid was intensive from the start and the rain of incendiaries resulted in a dash into the streets, and to roof-tops by fire-watchers.

DIVE ATTACKS

But as these were put out it was seen that one or two buildings were not so well equipped. In some offices bright windows showed that incendiaries inside the building were not being attended to.

It was the signal for the first of a long succession of dive attacks, and the planes appeared to be roaring down from the sky at a terrific speed, and there followed on each occasion a series of explosions.

The fire thus spread and increased with immense speed, and the heat became intense. It was impossible to approach some streets which had both sides ablaze.

When a store directly opposite my post was a great flame of fire, it was obvious that fire-watching had past beyond the practical stage.

3,000 BREAKFASTS

The raid affected some of the arrangements for the homeless, but others remained almost intact.

During the night several additional mobile Y.M.C.A. canteens and one of the U.S. ambulances arrived in the town.

The former were greatly appreciated by great numbers of police and fire officers.

By 10 o'clock on Saturday morning 3,000 breakfasts had been provided.

One of the hospitals put into effective operation plans for the evacuation of patients as a result of recent night raids. The institution was used only for the reception of casualties. Fires had been extinguished when thousands of people arrived in the town for business in the morning.

But some of the business features of the town were no more than shells or gaping wrecks.

SURGEON'S ESCAPE

An R.M.C. officer, one of the town's best known surgeons arriving in the town on leave, described the night as the worst he had experienced.

He was in the last war.

He and a small party were fortunate to escape from the basement of a store which was completely gutted by fire above them.

In the early stages, he had seen only one light in this vicinity, and the outbreak spread at a terrifying pace. At the report centres there was warm praise for the intrepid work of the boy messengers during a terrifying night.

FOOD OFFICES DESTROYED

Schools used as food offices have gone. One of the cinemas was damaged. Several restaurants have "disappeared." So too have shops and offices. There were other buildings which had very narrow escapes, having several bombs around them.

The attack began shortly after dark, and as in the previous nights' raids, fires provided beacons for the following waves of raiders.

There were numerous "incidents" reported, with incendiary bombs too numerous to record.

CASUALTIES

The casualties are not expected to be high having regard to the size of the raid, but no figures are yet available. Numbers of homeless are temporarily accommodated in halls or houses. Many voluntarily moved away.

Document 5: Official Report on the 'Three Nights' Blitz' by Mr Howell Lang Lang-Coath, Air Raid Precautions Controller for Swansea, to the Council of the County Borough of Swansea, 18 March 1941 (Swansea City Archives Office, P/SM 95 (County Borough of Swansea, A.R.P. Miscellanea)).

[fo. 1] **PRIVATE & CONFIDENTIAL**

COUNTY BOROUGH OF SWANSEA.

AIR RAIDS ON SWANSEA

19th, 20th and 21st February, 1941.

TRANSCRIPT OF SHORTHAND NOTES OF THE AIR RAID PRECAUTIONS CONTROLLER'S[1] STATEMENT to the COUNCIL on the 18th MARCH, 1941.

I am instructed by the Air Raid Precautions Committee to make a Report to you with regard to the enemy attacks here on the nights of the 19th, 20th and 21st February, 1941.

Swansea was faced with a teriffic ordeal on these three consecutive nights, in the heavy enemy attacks, with the latest technique of aerial bombardment by way of Incendiary and High Explosive bombs alternately, accompanied with dazzling, almost stationary flares dangling in the sky.

That ordeal was all the greater when it is realised that the results of the attacks on the first and second nights respectively had rendered considerable havoc in our midst, and had taxed the energies and resources of those engaged in combatting the attacks and dealing with the many difficulties which were left in their wake.

The third night, therefore, found those responsible for the defence of the town at some disadvantage in view of the ceaseless and tiring work they had performed on the two previous nights, when a few of us had had little sleep, and some of us are not quite as young as we were!

1. Howell Lang Lang-Coath was Town Clerk of Swansea from 1911 to 1943. He was appointed ARP Controller for the County Borough on 20 April 1939. For his actions as Controller he was awarded the CBE.

However, the personnel of the Civil Defence Organisation and the populace, I am pleased to say, stood up to that third night's ordeal with the same courage and with the same determination as on the previous nights. It is unnecessary for me, as the Air Raid Precautions Controller, to express [fo. 2] any opinion as to what was done, because better opinions than mine have been expressed, namely the opinion of the Minister of Health, Mr. Ernest Brown, who visited the Town, and Mr. William Mabane, M.P., the Parliamentary Secretary to the Minister of Home Security, representing his Minister in making a minute Inquiry here into the attacks and all appertaining to them, and consequent upon them, and the opinion they respectively expressed was that your Civil Defence Services had done magnificently. A similar opinion has been expressed by others eminently qualified to judge. I had not intended to mention these opinions, but, in view of the observations which have been made by some Members of the Council in regard to the Officials acting and carrying on during these dreadful times, and no Committees being called, I am compelled to do so to indicate how wrong and unfair those observations are. I do not, however, desire the Press to report this, it is private.

My difficulty this afternoon is not in telling you all about what has taken place, but in endeavouring to put it before you shortly and concisely. There is so much ground to cover.

The real satisfaction gained from all we have learned and all we have endured is through preparedness. The A.R.P. Committee and it's Chairman and the Officials have been preparing in anticipation of an ordeal like this for many months.

I do not suppose it could be realised here the times we have had to go to Cardiff, some-times with the Chairman,[1] sometimes without him – when [fo. 3] matters have been important on policy he has had to come – the times the Regional Commissioner [2] has been to Swansea – and I do not suppose the Council can realise the many hours that have been put in in preparing and anticipating all eventualities possible and devising all manner of things to meet situations which we endeavoured to visualise as likely to arise.

1. Alderman Percy Morris, J.P. (1893–1967). A member of the Council since 1927, by profession, he was a railway clerk for the Great Western Railway, which he joined in 1908. He was an active trade unionist, rising to become President of the Railway Clerks' Association of Great Britain and Ireland, 1943–53, and was Labour M.P. for Swansea West, 1945–59. He became Chairman of the ARP Committee when it was established in February 1938, and he remained active in Welsh ARP matters throughout the war.

2. Sir Gerald T. Bruce.

All forethought procurable has been made use of, and all information available has been considered and implemented where applicable, and when you see the amount of information that comes down from London and other places which has to be dissected, disseminated and used, it is amazing. No stone has been left unturned in doing our very best to cope with all that we could think of in what was coming to us, and in carrying out the instructions of the Chairman and of his A.R.P. Committee.

Mr. Mayor and Gentlemen can you just realise the position of affairs here on that Saturday morning? We had had three nights of a most terrible ordeal. You should sit in that Control Room – hear all those reports coming in – hear all the terrible things that are happening. I can assure you it is not a sinecure – it is a very responsible position, and one which I would rather not go through again. The other Officials can speak for themselves, but I am there in that room, Mr. Mayor and Gentlemen, and I know what is going on. I can imagine part of Swansea falling down, I can't go out to see for myself, but there it is, and it is a very apprehensive position to be in, and one in which you feel your position very acutely.

What did we find on that Saturday morning? Roads damaged and impassable. Sewers damaged. Electric cables and equipment damaged. 15 Schools destroyed or seriously damaged. Telephonic communication cut off. A Casualty List, fortunately and providentially not as large as might be
[fo. 4] expected. Over 6,500 people without a home to be dealt with.

The Food Office completely demolished, and all papers, books and records therein destroyed and lost. As a result, thousands of Food Registrations had gone, concerning consumers and not only in Swansea but outside of Swansea trading in the Town. The Town's Shopping Centre wiped out, including the Market. Shops rendered useless by being destroyed by bombs or being burned out, or by having delayed action bombs in front of them.

171 Food Shops gone – 64 Grocers, 61 Butchers, 12 Bakers and 34 Hotels Restaurants and Cafes gone. This figure does not deal with the Green Grocers and other Stalls in the lost market, but to illustrate to you from the Market point of view, there were 43 Butchers' Holdings in the Market and those 43 Butchers were supplying no less than 22,000 customers.

Gas and water cut off, causing lack of cooking arrangements to others in their homes who were not homeless.

St. Mary's church and other places of Worship destroyed.

Dangerous buildings required immediate attention. The Blitzed area had to be cordoned around. Rescues unfortunately still had to be made. The dead had to be identified, and they had to be buried. Numerous questions had to be answered. That, Gentlemen, was the position when one walked into this building at 9 o'clock on the Saturday morning after those terrible nights.

Whose responsibility was it? The law says it is the Controller's responsibility. The position was this – it just wanted a match lighting on to the material present to cause consternation and panic, and to put everything [fo. 5] in hopeless muddle and disorder, as had happened, so I am informed, in other towns in which it took some weeks to clear up, and from which towns people were seen wandering to districts outside, homeless and starving.

Might I deviate just one moment and go back to the Control Room,[1] because I want you to appreciate that the Control Room is the "Nerve Centre" of everything. When these Raids are going on everything comes through the Control Room, and if that Control Room is efficiently and properly administered, it can deal not only with the events that are then happening, but it can make provision for what has to be done in view of the knowledge which has obtained there of what is going on outside, and it is highly important, therefore, that the Control Room should be administered in the most accurate and efficient manner.

During the recent Blitz everything in the Control Room was kept on a level keel – perfect order – perfect coolness, and on the three nights no less that 8,000 messages were dealt with in that Control Room, and no less than 561 incidents were reported, and I have not yet heard one single complaint of any sort or kind in regard to the work done in the Control Room on those nights.

Information came through at all times from the Wardens, from the Police and all the Services, and indeed even from outside sources.

1. The Control Room was housed in the Green Room which was located behind the stage area of the Brangwyn Hall at the Guildhall.

As Controller may I say that I had a thorough picture throughout this dreadful period of the incidents which were reported from time to time, and I was well aware, in view of the help which I was receiving from my A.R.P. Officer and from all my co-Officials who were represented in the [fo. 6] Control Room, of the resources I had at my disposal during and subsequent to the Raids.

May I just give you an example of the kind of things which were receiving consideration, in addition to dealing with the incidents and general routine work of the Control Room itself.

We foresaw there was probability of trouble arising in regard to food supply. In the early hours of the morning my A.R.P. Officer telephoned through to the War Room at Cardiff for Mobile Canteens. Mr. Gealer,[1] my Deputy Food Executive Officer had the foresight to come in at 2.30 a.m. had a talk with me about the food position, and as a result of that talk we telephoned the Divisional Food Control Office at Cardiff forthwith. They were open at that hour of the morning. The result – soon after 9 o'clock on Saturday morning 16 Mobile Canteens were in operation in this town. This was done because Mr. Gealer came in, and we were able to discuss, in the Control Room, the position as we then knew it.

We found out on one occasion that the Hospital had been hit. Instructions were given to deflect all cases from the Hospital. Send them to Cefn Coed,[2] send them to Tawe Lodge,[3] and might I say here that this town is greatly indebted to both these places for the wonderful work they carried out.

Homeless – contacted the Public Assistance Officials at their homes to open the Rest Centres and to have them in readiness for those poor things

1. S.J. Gealer, A.I.M.T.A. was the Assistant Borough Treasurer, who had been loaned on secondment to Swansea's Food Control Committee.

2. Cefn Coed psychiatric hospital had opened in 1932, the first of Swansea's four great municipal undertakings of the 1930s. In February 1941, a number of psychiatric patients were transferred to the hospital at Bridgend, thereby making room available for war casualties. During the 'Three Nights' Blitz', 180 civilian casualties were admitted, mainly to the Princess Royal Wards (T.G. Davies, *A History of Cefn Coed Hospital* (Swansea, 1982)).

3. Tawe Lodge (later, Mount Pleasant Hospital) had originally been a Poor Law infirmary located in the Swansea Workhouse at Mount Pleasant. It became known as Tawe Lodge when the workhouse closed in 1930.

who had been bombed out, and even at that time commenced preparations for evacuation.

Rescue Parties – carefully surveying all our resources and arranging for reserves of Services of Rescue Parties – we were able to get Rescue Parties into Swansea from outside.

[fo. 7] Got in touch with the Military to get Military assistance in.

Working in conjunction with the Chief Constable[1] in regard to A.F.S. and matters which we wanted to inform him about.

Last, but not least, we were in constant communication with the Regional Commissioner in Cardiff, through whom we derive outside assistance.

This is a list of things which were happening in addition to the routine work of the Control Room.

The electric light failed, and the telephone failed. They had to be dealt with. Fortunately we had our emergency lighting, which had been approved by the A.R.P. Committee.

With regard to failure of the telephones – we had the Messenger Service[2] there ready to take the place of telephones. All these things were done in addition to the various messages which came through from time to time. As I have already said I cannot emphasise to you the importance of that Control Room.

It was very obvious during the third night that something had to be done. About 4 a.m. on the Saturday morning I contacted, through my A.R.P. Officer, every Corporation Official concerned. The message was for them

1. Frank Joseph May was Chief Constable from 1931 until his retirement in September 1941, when he was appointed Fire Force Commander of no. 21 Area of the newly constituted National Fire Service. This Area covered the Swansea District. He received the OBE for his work during the 'Three Nights' Blitz'.

2. The Messenger Service comprised mainly young teenage boys, supported by members of Boy Scout Troops. They carried messages on foot or by bicycle and their work involved them in frequently entering danger zones. Three of them were killed during the 'Three Nights' Blitz'. There was also a separate police Messenger Service.

to get out into the Blitzed area as soon as possible, so that we could hold a Meeting of Officials at 11 a.m. on Saturday morning to decide the best way to deal with the situation, and so I reported to The Mayor[1] what I had done at the first possible opportunity.

Before I leave the Control Room and before I come to the steps which
[fo. 8] were subsequently taken, which, perhaps is the most important matter, I want, if I may Mr. Mayor, to pay tribute, I cannot pay too high a tribute, to the work of your A.R.P. Officer, Mr. Brayley.[2] I do not know when he does go to bed, but I suppose he goes sometimes. I was able to accomplish all I have done by using the profound knowledge which Mr. Brayley possesses of A.R.P. work and A.R.P. personnel, and also the working of the Control Room. He has never failed to prompt me when I have wanted information. He has kept a cool head throughout, and his devotion to duty has been marvellous, and I cannot pay too high a tribute to the excellent work he has done.

We will leave the Control Room now, and go back to what was done to meet the situation.

At 11 o'clock on Saturday morning the Officials met, and the Mayor was good enough to come in. Although many of us had been without sleep for three nights, we were wonderfully awake, and sat down to deal with the whole position. The Mayor was there, and he can tell you what took place.

We dealt with matters as best we could. Roads, sewers and electric cables, etc., were reported on. In regard to these matters the Officials concerned, Mr. Heath[3] and Mr. Blackiston,[4] had already got going. In regard to electricity, extraordinary progress was made, and all I need to say to show what was done, notwithstanding the extensive damage, over 99% of the small consumers had their electric light without interruption. Any of the Services which were then out of commission were being put into commission as speedily as possible.

1. Councillor Thomas James, J.P., the member for the Sketty Ward.
2. Edwin J. Brayley replaced Captain E.B. Backhouse as ARP Officer in March 1940. He was awarded the MBE for his services during the 'Three Nights' Blitz'.
3. J.R. Heath, M.Inst.M. and Cy.E., Borough Engineer and Surveyor.
4. H.E. Blackiston, M.I.E.E., Chief Engineer and Manager for Swansea Corporation's Electricity Department.

Telephones – we dealt with this difficulty as quickly as we could by getting the Telephone Exchange on to the work.

[fo. 9] Then, we had 6,537 homeless people to deal with. Mr Saunders[1] has taken up his important work of billeting. He had already, in accordance with arrangements made before the Blitz, been very busy in finding Billets for those rendered homeless on the first two nights, and in due course, he found billets for all the others. In other words he, together with certain help from the Public Assistance Officer, found homes for no less than 6,537 people.

In the meantime your Rest Centres had been got into operation. Mr. Mayor and Gentlemen, might I pause just a moment with regard to the Rest Centres. For the information of those who do not know the details of them, might I say that in pursuance of the policy which has been outlined by the Committee, there exists 61 Rest Centres in the County Borough of Swansea, which covers, as you know, approximately 25,000 acres. 19 of these Rest Centres were in commission during this period. The Rest Centres have an attendant for each Centre. As soon as information is available in the Control Room as to the district which is affected by bombardment, it is given to the Public Assistance Officer,[2] and, through him to his Assistants, Mr. Shufflebotham[3] and Mr. Jones, who have worked extremely hard and very effectively with these Rest Centres.

In each of the Centres there is a small iron meal, which is kept, as no elections are now on, in ballot boxes, and consists of tea, canned milk, a little sugar and a few biscuits, so that directly the homeless people arrive at the Rest Centre there is a hot drink for them.

Then, of course, by the Organisation which is superintended over by Mr. Cann,[4] that is your Feeding Centres, they get a hot breakfast at 9.20–9.30
[fo. 10] a.m. and a hot dinner mid-day. That is how these Rest Centres operate. I

1. D. Ivor Saunders, F.S.I., Chartered Surveyor, was the Borough Estate Agent and Valuer who also had, in war time, the function of Billeting Officer.

2. The Public Assistance Officer at this time was Mr. G. Thomas.

3. W.E. Shufflebotham was Superintendant Relieving Officer in Swansea Corporation's Public Assistance Department, Mr. Jones being one of the Assistant Relieving Officers.

4. C. Cann had been employed in the Corporation's Committee Secretariat before being given responsibility for supervision of Feeding Centres.

believe that one or two days they did not get a hot dinner, because of the gas and water breakdown, but they had a good cold one.

Now we come to the Food Office.[1] The Food Office had gone. Mr Gealer and I, and the Chairman of the A.R.P. Committee had discussed long ago what would happen if at any time the Food Office did go, and we decided that the best thing to do was to re-establish the office here at the Guildhall until we found another office, so at 9 o'clock on the Saturday morning the Food Office opened at the Guildhall. Mr. Gealer had discussed with me the preservation of certain vital documents. We had duplicates of those documents made, and they were in the Guildhall in the Strong-Room. These duplicates were immediately got out, and the Food Office commenced to function.

The Food Traders and catering establishments which I have told you about were, most of them, destroyed, and the water and gas services prevented the public from cooking. Bakers could not operate, or could only operate in a very small way by hand. I have told you that Mr. Gealer came into the Control Room at 2.30 on the Saturday morning, and I told you that we arranged for Mobile Canteens. We also, with the assistance of the Area Bread Officer, obtained 10,000 loaves on the Saturday morning.

The Civil Defence Services had to be fed – provision having been made for them by the keeping in stock of iron rations. Many people from outside who had come in to assist – and the Military also had to be fed. The people at the Docks had to be fed, and many others. They were all looked after, and the Mobile Canteens were kept going, and I think it is only right Mr.
[fo. 11] Mayor and Gentlemen, that I should say that too high a tribute could not be paid to Mr. Gustavus for what he did in helping these people, and Mr. Sullivan. They have both done marvellous work – and they have both been written to, but I think it is fair that some special resolution should be passed putting on record our thanks to them both.

We had to relax the registration system in regard to food, and we used all the common sense we possibly could to attack the position, and to see that food was available.

The traders who had got food were asked to assist in every way they could, and we sent out information telling traders who were able to operate

1. The Food Office was situated in Northampton Place, in the centre of the main bombed area.

to assist others. Additional supplies were made available by various means which I need not deal with now. Wholesalers who were operating supplied retailers who were still able to trade. Our reserves of stocks which were available were used, and, to put it quite shortly, the Food Office, under the direction of Mr. Gealer acted as a Provision Centre, and generally the arrangements we had made to meet a very difficult food situation have stood the acid test of public approval. Here again it is only fair that credit should go where credit is due, and I desire to pay a tribute, and a very great tribute indeed to the magnificent work of Mr. Gealer. He not only worked, but he suggested, and did marvellous things to get this food position safe.

Now, coming to the matter upon which I desire confirmation. After conferring with the Mayor and the Chairman of the A.R.P. Committee, I opened, with the assistance of Mr. Cann and Mr. Gealer, two Cafes, one at Nelson Terrace and the other at the Workmen's Club, Alexandra Road, because we found many people who, although they had not been bombed [fo. 12] out and were able to work, had no means of getting meals. Meals were, and still are, being supplied at these Cafes. Dinners are served for 8d adults, 4d children, and anybody who hasn't got any money – a free meal.

The total number of meals which we provide at the present time is upwards of 1,600/1,700 a day. Sometimes up to 2,000 and about 1,000 meals are being prepared in these Cafes. The work of organising these Cafes has been done by Mr. Cann, and he has done really excellent work.

The Mobile Canteens also came in, as I have told you, to help, and Mrs. T.J. Rees, the Organiser of the Women's Voluntary Service, with her staff, rendered yeoman service in getting the kitchen in the Guildhall going, from which a quantity of food was prepared to be loaded into the Mobile Canteens for sending around the Borough and the Y.M.C.A., rendered similar service.

We experienced a difficulty in getting boiling water, and a local butcher placed his boilers at the disposal of those loading the Vans. I haven't got his name, but he placed his boilers at our disposal, and that is how the people concerned got their hot water.

Volunteers from the Food Office Staff stoked the boilers in the Guildhall, and the result was that there was a constant supply of boiling water, which enabled the canteens to keep going.

The Canteens operated under the direction of Mr. Gealer, and the closest possible liaison was established between myself and the Police, with the result that the vans were sent to the places where they were most needed. In [fo. 13] addition we were able to obtain 10 tons of cigarettes to send round the Borough to the various Services, and others.

With regard to the Market – this was completely destroyed, but in a few days Mr. Saunders set up a new Organisation which is now functioning in the United Welsh 'Bus Station in Singleton Street. We went through there last week with Major Gwilym Lloyd George, the Parliamentary Secretary to the Minister of Food, and it was surprising how well it was working, and how things were progressing.

Although we have been able to accomplish these things on the recent occasion, it is not going to be so easy if there is another Blitz, because, as you know, our resources are diminishing.

The Gas and Water situation was very difficult. Gas which is supplied by the Gas Company, we have no control over, and all that one could do there was to contact the Regional Commissioner. He is seeing to the question of gas repairs in his own way, and with the advice of his own engineers.

The Water position was very difficult, and was a position which caused a good deal of anxiety, because, as you will appreciate, public morale must be maintained. No less than 57 Public Watermains were damaged – amongst these being the 17" and 9" mains feeding Townhill Reservoir. Then the 12" main taking the water out of the same reservoir was also damaged. The 24" main and 18" main feeding Cwmdonkin Reservoir, and a large area en route, was also damaged, and the 14" and 12" mains on Cwmdonkin Supply in the town area were damaged too. Therefore, as a result of all this, a considerable portion of the Borough was in great [fo. 14] difficulty with regard to water supply. I believe upwards of 50 of these breaks have been repaired under great difficulty, because, as you know, the men cannot work very well in the night, in the blackout. However, I think all the Mains will soon be put in order once again, and in operation.

We dealt with the Water situation in this way. We got in touch with the Regional Commissioner, and with his help and the help of the Minister of Transport and the Military Authorities, 22 tank lorries came into the

Borough for the purpose of distributing water to consumers. We got 8 tanks for storage purposes at different centres, and no less than 1,800 tons of water was distributed in this way, and no less than 3,000 miles was covered in making this distribution, so you can just imagine the great work which was done in regard to keeping the water situation going.

In the meantime the following Public Works Contractors:–

Mr. E.J. Large – Agent to Messrs. Howard Farrow, Ltd.,
London and Killay, and
Mr. J.C. Church – South Wales Contractors, Ltd.,

got into touch with Mr. Hassall,[1] and gave considerable help to the Corporation by way of supply of expert labour and material.

Also we had now contacted the Military and 100 Pioneers were sent down, but they were not accustomed to digging, and were not a very big help, but they did their best.

The Staff and the Workmen in the Department of the Water Engineer worked terribly hard, and I am sure you are very much indebted to them for all that they have done.

[fo. 15] Rescue Work speaks for itself. You know all that has been done. Here again the efforts of both Mr. T.C. Prosser[2] and Mr. E.V. Bevan were wonderful, and indeed all the men who were working under them were the same. They never spared themselves and they worked almost to a standstill.

With regard to burials. There were considerable casualties, as you know, and the Parks Superintendent[3] says he still has a number of open graves, which I hope will never be required again.

1. J. Hassall, M.I.C.E. Chartered Civil Engineer, was the Borough Water Engineer and Manager.

2. T.C. Prosser was the Deputy Officer in Charge of Rescue, and was later awarded the BEM.

3. Mr. T. Winchcombe.

The Information Bureau came down, and opened an Office, and information could be obtained in regard to

Food	Assistance Board
Food – Salvage of	Retail Supplies
War Damage	Ministry of Food
Billeting	Ministry of Information
Ration Cards	Ministry of Labour
Identity Cards	&c.

On the Saturday afternoon, Mr. Armer, the Chairman of the Welsh Board of Health, came down, and also Colonel Sir Gerald T. Bruce, the Regional Commissioner. They were here shortly after 3 o'clock, and I had ready for them a short report telling them what had been done, and what was proposed to be done, and all I can tell you, Mr. Mayor and Gentlemen, is that they had no criticism to offer upon my Report.

I am sure the Council would like to know that much work has been done in regard to alleviation of distress. I am not very familiar with the details of this work because it has been taken on by the Mayor, but from what I do know of it, and if I were to try and make an estimate (and I do not want the
[fo. 16] press to report this,) I should say the amount of money already given out in distress in Swansea, through the Mayor's Fund, in conjunction with the Public Assistance Board, would be somewhere in the region of £50,000 – but, as I say, the Mayor is dealing with all this. If needs be he will use his own discretion when he talks to you about it.

Lord and Lady Plymouth came down to inspect the area. Lady Colefax, the Secretary of the British War Relief Society of America came with them, and offered the Mayor a considerable amount of clothes – which the Mayor accepted.

The Duke and Duchess of Beaufort also came down, and expressed great satisfaction with all that had been done.

Lord Horder and Miss Ellen Wilkinson, M.P., the Shelter Experts also came down, and likewise expressed satisfaction.

There have been various Deputations. Many letters of sympathy have been received – they will be mentioned to you to-day, from neighbouring authorities.

The most important visit of all was the Inquiry which Mr. William Mabane, M.P., held on the Saturday-week after the Blitz. He, as stated, came here to represent the Minister of Home Security, Mr. Herbert Morrison – accompanied by the Regional Commissioner, Colonel Sir Gerald T. Bruce, and Brigadier General Evans, V.C. They were met at the Guildhall by the Members of Parliament, the Chairman of the A.R.P. Committee, myself, as A.R.P. Controller, and all the Officials concerned. Those are the people he asked that should meet him. He did not want anybody else. He detailed those he required to see.

I told you at the outset of my Report Mr. Mabane was pleased with the way Swansea had managed it's own affairs, and this without outside assistance or intervention. I reported to him that the guns had ceased to fire o. 17] from 8.20 p.m. to 9.5 p.m. on the Friday night, and that this was the crucial period, and that the Officer in Charge of the Guns had reported to the Mayor and myself that he had ceased to fire on instructions.[1]

I cannot give you any information now on this very important and indeed delicate matter, excepting to say that it is being taken up in the appropriate quarter, and also the question that Swansea was considerably below it's quota in regard to the number of guns available on the nights of the 19th, 20th and 21st February, 1941.

Putting the position quite shortly, you have seen yourselves in the papers what Mr. Mabane has said, and it is that he considers it was a marvellous achievement.

In conclusion I wish to say that I have a duty cast upon me as Controller to act in an emergency. If you want me to remain as Controller – it is a voluntary office – it is unpaid – I shall be glad to do so for the sake of my town, and for the sake of those who are in it, but it is very discouraging, when one has done one's best, and when one has been told by experts that things are satisfactory, to have it suggested, that on Saturday morning at 9 o'clock, with all that was facing me, and having gone through the responsibility of those terrible three nights, when you think of all the damage, and all the deaths and all that is falling in the trail of those bombers, to have it suggested that I should have taken instructions in regard to calling a Committee. What for? What could they have done? I carried

1. The anti-aircraft barrage control centre received a hit on the night in question, and there was also night fighter activity above the town.

out my instructions to act in an emergency, and if there had been any Committees or any interruption, I can tell you, quite frankly, I could not
[fo. 18] have acted. I was too over-wrought – I had to keep a cool head and do my best, and my work has been approved by the Powers that be and all concerned.

I wish to say now, if I may, that I was supported most loyally by every Official of the Corporation. They were unstinting in their desire to give me information and help, and indeed encouragement. They rallied around me and did all in their power to assist me in dealing with the situation that Saturday morning. When I remind you now that it is nearly three weeks since these Blitzes occurred and that we have worked every day and worked practically every hour of the day – there is not much time to deal with Inquiries or Meetings which can be avoided.

I am your Servant – I am carrying out your instructions, and all I have done is to implement the policy and the direction of the A.R.P. Committee and it's Chairman, and the prescribed instructions upon which I am appointed Controller of Swansea.

I am proud to hold that position, and I am proud to have had the opportunity of working with the Officials who have worked with me and helped me to carry this thing through, and I think it is a great result to Swansea that we have got out of this as well as we have done.

I can only express my thanks to them – and if the policy adopted on this occasion is to continue, then I will be only too happy to do all I can to repeat what I have been able to do with the help of those who have assisted me on the last occasion. I earnestly trust, however, that that occasion will not arise.

Document 6: Mass-Observation Report on Swansea after the 'Three Nights' Blitz' (Tom Harrisson Mass-Observation Archive, University of Sussex Library, File Reports 595).

[fo. i]

Report from
Mass – Observation
on
SWANSEA

I. Introduction and description of damage.
II. Factors affecting Morale.
III. Discussion of General Morale.

SUMMARY OF CONCLUSIONS:

The morale of Swansea is good. People are inevitably shaken underneath their surface of good morale. But the co-operativeness of the Swansea people and the comparative efficiency of the emergency organisation seems to have enabled people to bear up under conditions involving the temporary loss of all public utilities. The fact that the centre of the town is roped off on account of time bombs, so that the exact extent of the damage cannot yet be seen, has probably also helped. There are no special complaints among Swansea people, except at a speech on the wireless describing them as smiling and ignoring the raids. But actually there was one big inefficiency, the distribution of information. The efficiency of services must have been reduced by the fact that many people did not know where to go or what to do about the various problems. Attention to non-material factors such as this, and the impossibility of buying cigarettes when nerves were shaking, would ease the strain which the population of a blitzed town much inevitably experience.

From
82, Ladbroke Road,
London. W.11.

1st March, 1941.

[fo. 1]

M–O
1.3.41.

Report on SWANSEA

I. *INTRODUCTION & DESCRIPTION OF DAMAGE.*

On the nights of Wednesday, Thursday and Friday, the 19th, 20th and 21st February, Swansea experienced heavy raiding. On Sunday 23rd February an investigation of the general effects of these raids on morale was undertaken by a single investigator. Since only one investigator was involved, this report cannot be compared directly with earlier reports on blitzed towns in which several investigators were involved. But the experience gained in the investigation makes it possible to interpret the things observed in terms of morale, in a way which would not have been possible without more elaborate investigation in the case of earlier blitzes.

Damage (This is for the purpose of forming a background to the report only)

The first two raids were chiefly on residential areas away from the centre of the town, the third on the centre of the town itself. In addition to H.E. and incendiaries, an abnormally large number of delayed action bombs were dropped. Thus, on Saturday the whole of the centre of the town was roped off and no entry allowed. Bombs had also fallen fairly uniformly over a considerable residential area surrounding the town centre, and there had been particularly severe bombing at Pennycraig,[1] a council house estate towards the borders of the town. The docks appeared to have escaped serious bombing.

Damage in the town centre was very considerable. It was estimated that 50% of the buildings in this area were demolished, and there were numerous delayed action bombs still unexploded. The damage in Pennycraig was even worse. But in the rest of the town the damage was scattered, and South-west of the railway station was almost untouched. The Civic Centre was on the border between the part completely untouched and the part which had experienced scattered bombs, and had itself escaped completely.

1. This is a reference to Mayhill.

As a result of the first two nights' bombing, people had gone to shelters in the centre of the town for the third night, and had been in the thick of the bombing.

II. *FACTORS AFFECTING MORALE* (Approximate situation only)

(a) *Public Utilities.*

[fo. 2] Light, power, water, gas, telephone and transport were all interfered with seriously in the bombed area. These gradually came back during the next few days, but on Wednesday 26th February it was estimated that 30% of bombed area was still without light, 50% without water, all without gas. And transport and telephones were still seriously interfered with.

Water was thoroughly inadequate for housewives who never had enough to wash in. Probably 25% of the people did not know that water from carts was available.

Out of town 'buses were coming as far into the town as they could, but there were no in-town 'buses running, and the service was quite inadequate although extra 'buses had been pressed into service. A 'bus inspector said that there was nothing for the 'buses to come in for, and that the only people using them were sightseers, but this is probably an exaggeration.

The absence of gas meant that housewives were unable to cook, which creates a demand for tinned food.

(b) *Food*

There were the usual difficulties about *food supply*, but in Swansea these were not as severe as in some other blitzed towns. The chief shortage was of tinned foods, and of things which could be eaten without cooking. Rationed foods and meat were in sufficient supply. The only thing which was almost unobtainable was tobacco. Shopkeepers and housewives alike, however, were using their reserves, and there seemed a possibility that there would be a delayed shortage of some things if further supplies were not forthcoming.

The food situation was greatly eased by the expedition with which *Emergency Ration cards* were issued, for use at any shop. It probably means that supplies were good that in spite of these emergency cards, the number of shops destroyed, there was no real shortage of rationed goods.

The only hitch in the working of the scheme was that some people did not know that emergency ration cards could be obtained or where to obtain them.

Another factor easing the situation was the prompt organisation of *canteens and mobile feeding centres*. Those organised by the Town Council were closed on Tuesday evening, their place being taken by two cafeterias for hot meals. In general, organised feeding centres were well organised immediately after the raids, and after a few days, found to be no longer necessary in large numbers. These again were well organised, and again the exception was the distribution of information about them. Within 400 yards of one cafeteria only ten out of 41 people knew of the existence of the cafeteria, those not knowing including three policemen and one WVS worker.

(c) *Shelters*

Swansea is quite well supplied with shelters from a quantitative point of
[fo. 3] view, but qualitatively all the good ones were in the heavily bombed centre of the town. Those outside were mostly surfact [*sic*] shelters of particularly bad quality. Thus, there are very few efficient shelters left in Swansea for present use. It was noticed that surfact [*sic*] shelters were rarely used, and even basement shelters were not being used extensively when observed. During the three nights of raid, people had migrated to the deep shelters in the centre, which had borne the brunt of the bombing on the last night.

(d) *Rest Centres and Official Evacuation*

The Rest Centres were numerous, and appeared to be well organised. There were an exceptional number of people in these owing to the large number of delayed action bombs. Organisation appeared to be sufficient to deal with these numbers, however, there being no exceptional food shortage although the amount of bedding was certainly not sufficient for the numbers who were said to have been in the Rest Centres immediately after the raids. The Rest Centres were quickly cleared by evacuation to surrounding towns and villages, so that by Wednesday there were few people except those waiting for unexploded bombs to go off. But with rest centres, too, it was found that the distribution of information about them was bad.

The situation was greatly helped by the Welsh habit of visiting friends and relatives. It is believed that besides the large numbers in the Rest Centres, a still larger number went to the houses which had not been bombed, or went there after a short stay in the rest centres which acted as a sort of clearing house.

A visit to Mumbles, a nearby town to which many people had evacuated both officially and unofficially, showed a great cooperation there. All the churches, halls, cinemas and even private houses had open doors so that people came in as they could.

(e) *Information*

The big breakdown in an otherwise efficient organisation was the *distribution of information*. The Civic Centre had not been destroyed and was able to cope reasonably satisfactorily with the many problems involved in a blitzed town, but in coping with these it seems to have forgotten to let people know what it was doing. A large number of police had been drafted in from outside, and they knew little of the town geography. Local police and wardens were not much better informed. Even at the Civic Centre it was impossible to find out much of the necessary information such as where the Rest Centres were. Repeated references have already been made to people who did not know of water carts and other services which had been provided.

There were two M.O.I. vans seen, but these were outside the Civic Centre when seen, not patrolling the streets. Only three information notices were seen, all telling where to go for War Damage compensation and tow
[fo. 4] *[sic]* of them within 50 yards of the offices concerned. Apart from the effect on morale of such lack of information, it seems certain that the value of the comparatively efficient organisation of services must have been considerably reduced by the fact that many people did not know where to find these facilities, or even that they existed. Several times the investigator was thanked for telling people he was conversing with what they should do about their ration cards.

General Note on material facts

Although Swansea suffered severely from damaged utilities, organisation was more nearly adequate to cope with the various problems than in most of the blitzed towns already studied. The Civic Centre is crowded by a continual stream of people, but the officials maintained a kind and patient manner. Undoubtedly the organisation was greatly helped by the co-operativeness of the people who had not been bombed, as exemplified by the people of Mumbles; and Swansea people seem to show a greater self-reliance than many of the people in English towns. As an example of what is involved in this organisation, the official in control of Feeding centres said that he had fed as many as 800 in one place at one time. It is probable, however, that if the distribution of information had been adequate, a still larger quantity of people would have had to be dealt with by the various services.

III. *DISCUSSION OF GENERAL MORALE*

Swansea, like other blitzed towns, showed several well defined after effects of the blitz. Gasmask carrying had increased, there were large crowds of sightseers, there was considerable unofficial evacuation, and a great deal of talk about air raids. These and other factors indicate that Swansea had been shaken by the raids, as it could not very well help being shaken. But in Swansea the effect appeared to have been no more than a [fo. 5] shaking (although a shaking likely to leave a permanent after effect on the general attitude). Morale was undoubtedly good. There was little rumour, practically no grumbling, and a considerable amount of joking. The talk about air raids was not obsessional. The attitude seemed to be that the thing had happened, and all that could be done was to make the best of it. But the extent to which people were shaken could sometimes be told, as in the case of a housewife, who after explaining that they had been managing on the supplies they had in the house for the time being, in a quite matter of fact way, added at the end of her remarks:

"I hope we don't get no more; it's awful isn't it?"

Or the people who did not jump at the sound of the explosions (which were frequent) of delayed action bombs, but made jokes about it; a reaction considerably better than open nervousness, but nevertheless showing an underlying tension.

Or the people who did not go to shelter when an air-raid warning sounded, but who stood in their doorways and laughed.

These are the signs of the tensions which lead to unofficial evacuation, high gasmask carrying, and so on, and which occur in all blitzed towns.

The difference between Swansea and towns showing less good morale seems to be chiefly that in Swansea people put a good face on things, whereas in some places the extent to which people are shaken shows more on the surface, although so far it has never been spoken aloud to any great extent. Swansea is more matter of fact.

Special Factors

[fo. 6] Public houses in Swansea form a good example of the way Swansea is bearing up under raids. Although a policeman said there were no pubs open, it was found that in all the partially bombed districts the pubs were not only open, but attendance was average. Nor was the talk exclusively about raids; scandal, jobs, etc. figuring also, though to a lesser extent in the conversations.

Unofficial evacuation has already been referred to. A councillor in charge of billeting at Mumbles summed up the attitude of the evacuees when he said:

"Firstly, they're frightened, definitely frightened, it's no good hiding that fact. Secondly, they do feel ever so much safer even though they're only five miles away. Thirdly they come from all sections of the community and all types. Oh, just as many men as women, yes, they're just as bad – yes, a large percentage are bombed out and have no home to go back to, but I wouldn't say most, we must be accurate. I just say a large percentatge."

It must always be remembered that it is the more scared who evacuate. These are also the ones who let the extent to which they are shaken be seen. With these should be compared the type of remark frequently heard among those staying behind:

"Oh well, we'll just have to grin and bear it."

In connection with evacuation, the practice of going to friends and relatives has probably been a stabilising factor. The person who has a relation who has been bombed is apt to spread stories of bombing more than the person who has experienced the bombs and probably the closer contact with the event caused by taking in the suffered has the effect of preventing these stories. The extent to which friends and relatives offered hospitality is shown by the following remark from a butcher who had sent [fo. 7] his family to relatives outside Swansea:

"There was my house standing empty, but do you think anyone would take it? No. I've offered it to three customers who were bombed out – oh, they were staying up here somewhere, in someone's house."

Or as another man proudly said:

"They all have relatives around somewhere, and if not anyone will put them up – that's the Welsh nature."

There was, however, some sleeping in fields by unofficial evacuees. This was attributed by one man to the fact that the villages were full of evacuees from London.

There were very few *rumours* heard, none of the Haw-Haw type. One rumour was that the shelters in the centre of the town were to be sealed up with bodies inside them, a rumour which seems to recur in different places when shelters are hit.

Grumbles were almost non-existent. This seems to be a tribute to the organisation of Swansea and the co-operativeness of its people. The only two grumbles heard were at a speech made by Mr. Attlee before the raids saying how good production was. Some people attribute the raids to this speech, according to a police officer. The other was in connection with the wireless talk after the blitz. A note is added on this at the end of the report.

The strain which such a raid produces comes to the surface occasionally, of course. A barber said:

"Oh yes, people were pretty good. On Saturday though I heard several people. 'If there was a vote taken, peace or war, we'd vote for peace' – men mostly. Yes peace at any price they were saying."

And a hotel waitress said:

"I ask you gentlemen, will this help to win the war – all this destruction, all these lovely buildings, all these people, what good does it do?"

These came perhaps from the people who evacuate – or do not only
[fo. 8] because they cannot.

One thing which may have an importance is that the badly damaged centre of the town is completely roped off, so that the extent of the damage cannot yet be seen by the people. The destruction of landmarks and shopping cnetres [*sic*] is always an important factor in affecting morale. The effect of such destruction was illustrated by the remark of one man:

"I mean to say, to me St. Mary's was Swansea. Admittedly I use the car park more than the church – I've only been inside it once in my life, but still, it's Swansea."

CONCLUDING DISCUSSION

It can thus be said that the co-operativeness of the people and the organisation of the Civic Centre aided by this has enabled Swansea to stand up fairly well to its heavy raids. There are weak spots in the morale, but on the whole it is undoubtedly good. Probably the roping off of the town centre while shock was at its highest has helped people to overcome the intital state of shock. It seems certain, however, that underneath the surface people are considerably shaken, and will need time to recover themselves at all completely. Something of this can be seen from the following impression of the investigator on arriving in Swansea:

First impression is vivid. Arrive 8.30 p.m. in the dark. Man outside: "No buses, no taxis, you can't go that way – the whole centre of the town is down."

Walk round for half an hour, ask people where I could sleep – no one knows – they talk in subdued voices and seem dazed. Fire hoses littering the streets – can just make out that most of the streets I'm walking down are only of empty shells at least, trip over a firehose and swear so loudly that it produces two policemen who go round with me another $^1/_2$ hour before finding the biggest hotel in the place – the Grand, by the station – which will take me in, although it has no windows, light and hardly any staff.

[fo. 9] Next morning the town is horribly quiet, although a bomb had just fallen and the dust not yet settled. People pad about the street – a man shouts a cheery greeting to another and it echoes back – people look at him as though it was in church.

By Tuesday either the investigator or the inhabitants were used to it.

From the material collected it seems certain that the change was as much in the people of Swansea as in the investigator. It was, for example, noted that the number of jokes made in the next days was particularly high, and although the proportion was perhaps *too* high for complete stability, the difference between this atmosphere and the one conveyed by the investigator's impression above is marked.

[fo. 10] *Note on Wireless Talk about Swansea*

Nearly everthing that need to be said about the talk by the editor of a Swansea paper on the wireless on Thursday night was said by the following Swansea man:

"He's buggered us this time hasn't he – oh, it is in a mess. But the people were marvellous, especially the women – they can take it all right. But not like that bloke said on the wireless on Thursday night – they don't go about smiling about it – the people who have lost friends and relatives, they don't go about grinning."

The talk, which was of the usual journalistic, nobody-even-noticed-it type, was an insult to the shaken people of Swansea who were suffering from severe strain in carrying on. They were behaving well *considering the circumstances*, and to describe them as behaving in the manner of people who were refusing to let the loss of sixpence worry them was bound to bring a torrent of abuse. Swansea people resented the talk because it took away from their genuine efforts all semblance of reality in order to give it an artificial glamour. They knew they couldn't possibly have behaved in the way they were described as behaving, and resented being made to feel they had fallen short of some ideal standard when they were doing their best. Such talks do not in the end even benefit the morale of people outside the area described, for when a new area suffers from severe raids, people unconsciously remember what they have heard, and lose confidence because they do not reach this standard of behaviour, which is an impossible ideal. To describe the Swansea people as behaving well may be a good thing; but only if the ideal so set up is one which it is humanly possible to attain.

Bibliography

PRIMARY SOURCES

A. Unpublished

Bundesarchiv/Militärarchiv, Freiburg

RL7/96. Oberste Truppenkommandobehörden der Luftwaffe: Lagemeldungen über den Luftangriff auf Swansea, fos. 14–22^{v}.

Public Record Office, London

ADM 199/64. Admiralty, War History Cases and Papers, Balloon defences.

ADM 199/66. Admiralty, War History Cases and Papers, Anti-aircraft defences of ports.

AIR 2/5063. Air Ministry, Registered Files, Casualties to enemy aircraft, 1939–41.

AIR 2/5245. Air Ministry, Registered Files, Night Fighter Squadrons.

AIR 2/7391. Air Ministry, Registered Files, Fighter Command Night Interceptions, 1940–2.

HO 186/536. Ministry of Home Security: Air Raid Precautions (ARP GEN) Registered Files, Regional Commissioner's Monthly Reports for Region 8.

HO 186/1259. Ministry of Home Security: Air Raid Precautions (ARP GEN) Registered Files, Inspector General's Reports, 1941–3.

HO 186/1820. Ministry of Home Security: Air Raid Precautions (ARP GEN) Registered Files, Civil Defence training.

HO 199/145. Ministry of Home Security, Intelligence Branch Registered Files, Air Raid, Swansea, 10/11 August 1940.

HO 199/152. Ministry of Home Security, Intelligence Branch Registered Files, Air Raid, Swansea, 17/18 January 1941.

HO 199/446. Ministry of Home Security, Intelligence Branch Registered Files, Monthly Morale Reports.

INF 1/174. Ministry of Information, Files and Correspondence, Broadcast Commentaries on the Effects of Air Raids.

INF 1/264. Ministry of Information, Files and Correspondence, Home Intelligence Daily Reports.

INF 1/536. Ministry of Information, Files and Correspondence, Home Intelligence Monthly Reports.

Somerset County Record Office, Taunton

C/CD/Gen Box 3/27. ARP Diary of Incidents for Somerset.

C/CD/Gen Box 6/64. ARP Register of Messages, December 1940–April 1941.

Southampton City Record Office

SC/CD2/1. File on air raids on Southampton.

Swansea City Archives Office

BA 2. Borough Architect, Files relating to the Guildhall.

BE 52. Borough Engineer, War Damage Files.

D 6. Local Press (see also Newspapers below).

D 32/1. List of air raids.

D 35. War-time diaries of Laurie Latchford, air raid warden in Swansea.

D 42. Documents relating to ARP in Swansea, 1940–3.

D 53. Papers of Percy Morris.

D 68/1. County Borough of Swansea, Auxiliary Fire Service Records.

D 235.	County Borough of Swansea, Auxiliary Fire Service, Photograph Album, April 1939–August 1941.
EA 50.	Borough Estate Agent, Letterbooks and Files.
EA 52.	Borough Estate Agent, War Damage Files.
FAC 151.	'Days of the Grasshopper. Swansea, January– February 1941', typescript translation by Alan Rees of Aneirin ap Talfan, *Dyddiau'r Ceiliog Rhedyn. Abertawe, Ionawr–Chwefror 1941* (Llundain, n.d. [1943]).
MP/Misc.	*Luftwaffe* Target Map of Swansea, 1941.
P/D 227.	Photographs of bomb damage, 1940–1.
P/PR 95.	Photographs of the Swansea air raids.
P/SM 95.	Miscellaneous material on the Swansea air raids.
TC 3.	Minutes of Council and Committees.
TC 51.	Town Clerk, Small Correspondence Files, Old Series.
TC 52.	Town Clerk, Small Correspondence Files, New Series.
TC 53.	Town Clerk, Old Correspondence Files, Large Format.
TC 55.	Town Clerk, Small Format 'A' Files.
TC 57.	Town Clerk, Correspondence, Miscellaneous.
TC 200.	Town Clerk, ARP property requisition files.

Tom Harrisson Mass-Observation Archive, University of Sussex Library

File Reports 595.

Topic Collection, Air Raids 10/S.

West Glamorgan County Archive Service, Swansea

D/D Z 126.	Diary of Will Thomas, air raid warden in St Thomas, Swansea, August 1940–September 1941.

B. Newspapers

Herald of Wales.
South Wales Evening Post.
Völkischer Beobachter.
Western Mail.

C. Published

BEKKER, C., *The Luftwaffe War Diaries* (New York, 1964).

HALDANE, J.B.S., *ARP* (London, 1938).

Hitler's War Directives, 1939–45, ed. H.R. Trevor-Roper (London, 1964).

Kriegstagebuch des Oberkommandos der Wehrmacht, ed. H.-A. Jacobsen (Frankfurt am Main, 1965).

LATCHFORD, L.,'Swansea at War: a Civilian Diary', serialised in the *South Wales Evening Post* (2, 3, 6, 9, 10, 13, 16, 17, and 20 September 1980).

MINISTRY OF INFORMATION/MINISTRY OF HOME SECURITY, *Front Line, 1940–1. The Official Story of the Civil Defence of Britain* (London, 1942).

MINISTRY OF HOME SECURITY, *Objects Dropped from the Air* (London, 1941).

TALFAN, Aneirin ap, *Dyddiau'r Ceiliog Rhedyn. Abertawe, Ionawr–Chwefror 1941* (Llundain, n.d. [1943]).

SECONDARY

ALBAN, J.R., *Air Raids on Swansea* (Swansea, 1981).

ALBAN, J.R., '*Blitzkrieg*, Phoenix from the Ashes', *Herald of Wales Special Commemorative Supplement on the 'Three Nights' Blitz'* (February 1991), vi–vii.

ALBAN, J.R., *Markets in Swansea* (Swansea, 1991).

ALBAN, J.R., 'Preparations for Air Raid Precautions in Swansea, 1935–9', *Morgannwg*, xxviii (1984), 55–73.

ALBAN, J.R., 'The Second World War', *The City of Swansea. Challenges and Change*, ed. R.A. Griffiths (Stroud, 1990), pp. 130–44.

ALBAN, J.R., 'A Town at War', *Western Mail* (21 August 1989), 8 and (22 August 1989), 12–13.

ARTHUR, N., *Swansea at War: a Pictorial Account, 1939–45* (Manchester, 1988).

BAUMBACH, W., *The Life and Death of the Luftwaffe* (New York, 1960).

BLACKSTONE, G., *History of the British Fire Service* (London, 1969).

CALDER, A., *The People's War. Britain, 1939–45* (London, 1969).

COLLIER, B., *The Defence of the United Kingdom* (London, 1957).

COPE,V., 'The Short Term Effects of the "Three Nights' Blitz" on Swansea, 19, 20, 21 February 1941' (unpublished BEd dissertation, College of St Paul and St Mary, Cheltenham, 1982).

DEIGHTON, L. and HASTINGS, M., *Battle of Britain* (London, 1980, repr. 1990).

The Guildhall, Swansea. Essays to Commemorate the Fiftieth Anniversary of its Opening, ed. J.R. Alban (Swansea, 1984).

HARRISSON, T., *Living through the Blitz* (London, 1976).

HUNT, W.W., *'To Guard my People'. An Account of the Origin and History of the Swansea Police* (Swansea, 1957).

IRVING, D., *The Rise and Fall of the Luftwaffe. The Life of Erhard Milch* (London, 1973).

JEFFERY, T., *Mass-Observation: a Short History* (Birmingham, 1978).

JOHNSON, B., *The Secret War* (London, 1978).

JONES, R.V., *Most Secret War* (London, 1978).

KILLEN, J., *History of the Luftwaffe* (London, 1966).

LONGMATE, N., *Air Raid. The Bombing of Coventry, 1940* (London, 1976).

MARWICK, A., *The Home Front* (London, 1976).

MASON, F.K., *Battle over Britain* (London, 1969).

MORRIS, J., 'Morale under Air Attack: Swansea, 1939–41', *Welsh History Review*, xi, no. 3 (1983), 358–87.

MUNSON, K., *German Aircraft of World War Two* (London, 1978).

MURRAY, W., *Luftwaffe. Strategy for Defeat, 1933–45* (London, 1985).

O'BRIEN, T.H., *Civil Defence* (London, 1955).

PILE, F., *Ack-Ack* (London, 1949).

PRICE, A., *Blitz on Britain* (London, 1976).

PRICE, A., *The Bomber in World War II* (London, 1976).

PRICE, A., *Luftwaffe Handbook, 1939–45* (London, 1977).

PRYER, K., *Luftwaffe over Swansea. A History of the Air Attacks on Swansea, 1939–45* (various editions, Swansea, n.d.).

RICHARDS, D. and SAUNDERS, H. St.G., *The Royal Air Force, 1939–45* (London, 1953).

ROBINS, N.A., *Eye of the Eagle. The Luftwaffe Aerial Photographs of Swansea* (Swansea, 1993).

SHERIDAN, D., *The Mass-Observation Records, 1937–49* (Brighton, 1981).

SMITH, J.R., KAY, A.L., and CREEK, E.J., *German Aircraft of the Second World War* (London, 1972).

SOUTH WALES EVENING POST, *Memories of Swansea at War* (Manchester, 1988).

[SPENCER, G.], *Catholic Life in Swansea. The Centenary of St David's Church, Swansea, 1847–1947* (Cardiff, n.d. [?1947]).

Swansea. An Illustrated History, ed. Glanmor Williams (Swansea, 1990).

THOMAS, N.L., *The Story of Swansea's Districts and Villages* (revised edn., Swansea, 1969).

THOMAS, N.L., *The Story of Swansea's Markets. A History of their early Beginnings down to the Present Day* (Neath, 1966).

TITMUSS, R.M., *Problems of Social Policy* (London, 1950).

TWYFORD, H.P., *It Came to Our Door* (Plymouth, 1946).

VÖLKER, K.-H., *Dokumente und Dokumentarfotos zur Geschichte der Deutschen Luftwaffe* (Stuttgart, 1968).

WAKEFIELD, K., *The First Pathfinders. The Operational History of Kampfgruppe 100, 1939–45* (London, 1981, repr. Somerton, 1992).

WALKER, D.G., *St Mary's Church, Swansea. A Short History of the Parish Church of Swansea* (3rd edn., Swansea, 1967).

WARD, A., *A Nation Alone. The Battle of Britain, 1940* (London, 1989).

WASLEY, G., *Blitz. An Account of Hitler's Aerial War over Plymouth in March 1941, and the Events that Followed* (Exeter, 1991).

WESTERN MAIL, *Bombers over Wales* (Cardiff, n.d.).